I0080009

Praises for

Your Journey to Truth

There are people all over this world dealing with the lies and deceptions of the enemy with acceptance. *"Called to Truth"* is a key ring packed tight with the tools you need to break free from the bondage that is keeping you from fulfilling your destiny. So many of us have absorbed many lies over the course of time that eventually transform to truth in our minds, and the study guide, *"Your Journey to Truth,"* is an amazing path to true freedom. In James 1:24, the Bible tells us that as humans we can quickly lose sight of who we are but *"Called to Truth"* and the study guide, *"Your Journey to Truth,"* forces you to dig deep into how you have landed where you are and provides the rope and light that you need to find your way out! We at Ultimate Faith Christian Center have included these resources in our School of Ministry Curriculum and are excited to see deliverance take place. If you want transformation in your life, renew your mind with *"Called to Truth"* and the study guide *"Your Journey to Truth."* You will not be disappointed.

—**Pastor David Jordan**, Senior Pastor, *Ultimate Faith Christian Center*

Denise White has written another amazing book as a study guide, *"Your Journey to Truth"*, to accompany her first book *"Called to Truth."* The entire study guide is completely Holy Spirit filled, and I know will give you what I call "Keys to the Kingdom!" When you are done with the study guide, you will be whole in your mind, body, spirit, and soul. You will know your identity in God, you will deepen your intimate relationship with Him, and be ready to step into that awesome destiny that God has preordained for your life!

—**Pastor Richard P. Schwoegler III**, Pastor Founder/President, *Surrender All To Jesus Ministries*

Denise White has thoughtfully and prayerfully produced this incredibly valuable tool to accompany her book *"Called to Truth"*. This study guide is exactly what you will need to dig deep and go beyond just reading another book. Her probing, insightful questions will cause you to pause and digest the truth within the pages of her book. You will be challenged and pressed to let your roots go deep into the application of God's Word. Be blessed as you dive deep and experience a new level of faith and fruit using this must have study guide.

—**Paula Wade**, Minister of the Gospel of Jesus Christ, Graduate of Charis Bible College

Your Journey to Truth

A Practical, Biblical Study Guide to Spiritual & Physical Wholeness

DENISE WHITE

Published by KHARIS PUBLISHING, imprint of KHARIS MEDIA LLC.

Copyright © 2021 Denise White

ISBN-13: 978-1-63746-106-8

ISBN-10: 1-63746-106-2

Library of Congress Control Number: 2021952580

All rights reserved. This book or parts thereof may not be reproduced in any form, stored in a retrieval system, or transmitted in any form by any means - electronic, mechanical, photocopy, recording, or otherwise - without prior written permission of the publisher, except as provided by United States of America copyright law.

All KHARIS PUBLISHING products are available at special quantity discounts for bulk purchase for sales promotions, premiums, fund-raising, and educational needs. For details, contact:

Kharis Media LLC
Tel: 1-479-599-8657
support@kharispublishing.com
www.kharispublishing.com

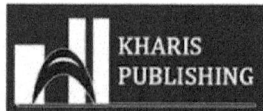

ACKNOWLEDGEMENT

———————◦✦◦———————

Thanks be to God for my victory through my Lord Jesus Christ! His truth has set me free! God has not given me a spirit of fear, but of power, of love, and of a sound mind.

Additionally, I am grateful to my husband, Jim, who told me early on to write a study guide for *Called to Truth, A Practical, Biblical Guide to Spiritual & Physical Wholeness*. I have treasured his support and encouragement throughout this process.

CONTACT INFORMATION

Email: dwhite.calledtotruth@gmail.com

DISCLAIMER

This study guide is not intended to provide medical advice or professional counseling. This study guide is not intended to take the place of medical treatment or professional counseling. Always consult with your medical health care provider or professional counselor before making any changes in your physical regimen regarding fasting, medication, diet, or any treatment. This study guide is not a substitute for medical care, advice, diagnosis, treatment, or professional counseling.

TABLE OF CONTENTS

PREFACE

This study guide accompanies "*Called to Truth: A Practical, Biblical Guide to Spiritual & Physical Wholeness.*" Come along on **Your Journey to Truth** to uncover the lies that steal your peace and destiny. My *Called to Truth* journey led to breakthrough in my life. The keys to my transformation were sorrowfully repenting (a change of mind) and confessing (agreeing with) the word of God. I had an incredible revelation of how I had striven in life with my own misguided ways and ended up broken before the LORD many times. This transformation process was a removal of lies and sin in my life that caused me to be deceived. As the Word of God shone on the dark places of my soul and mind, I was changed, and I will continue this sanctification process throughout my life.

As you move through the pages of *Your Journey to Truth*, prayerfully commit your steps to the LORD for His guidance and revelation as you follow the Holy Spirit, and the word of God. This Study Guide is a tool to help you move into your peace and destiny. First, it is important to enter *Your Journey to Truth* and travel through the pages of this study guide with sincerity and honesty. This journey is based on truth; to examine yourself with humility and honesty is necessary for breakthrough. Secondly, if you are married, I recommend you and your spouse go on this journey of truth together. Your spouse may be able to help bring something to light to which you are spiritually blind. Third, for individuals who will be doing this study by themselves, I recommend you have a trusted friend that you allow to speak into your life. There may be questions in this study guide to which you are spiritually blind about a situation or personal attribute. Therefore, if you have someone you trust to speak life and truth to you, you will be more likely to find the areas of deception and stumbling blocks in your life. Finally, allowing God into the secret places of your heart, and seeking Him humbly for truth, will change you forever. King David asked the LORD in Psalm 26:2 to test and examine his mind, will, and emotions and to refine him. This process will release out of your belly all the baggage you are holding onto in your heart and mind that hold you captive to lies. Recognizing and renouncing lies and filling yourself with truth will move you into His peace and your destiny.

PRAYER TO CONFESS JESUS AS YOUR LORD AND SAVIOR (It is important to pray out loud because you are making a confession of what you believe.)

I confess with my mouth that the Lord Jesus is the Son of God. Jesus Christ died on the cross for my sins and the sins of the world. Jesus Christ resurrected from the dead and will return one day. I am a sinner who needs Jesus as my Lord and Savior. Second Corinthians 7:10 says godly sorrow works repentance to salvation. I repent and ask you to cleanse me of all unrighteousness according to First John 1:9.

According to Romans 10:10, "For with the heart man believes to righteousness; and with the mouth confession is made to salvation." Jesus come into my life and lead me!

PRAISE GOD FOR YOUR DECISION TO SERVE AND FOLLOW HIM WITH YOUR WHOLE HEART!

CHAPTER 1

---◆◆◆---

CALLED TO TRUTH

Years ago, when we had settled into our home in Arizona, we started traveling up north in the summer to Pinetop-Lakeside. It was very lovely up there at an elevation of 6800 feet, with much cooler summers, beautiful Ponderosa pine trees, over 200 miles of hiking trails, and many lakes and streams. We stayed at this adorable, cozy cabin and made great family memories.

But there is one hiking adventure in one summer which we will never forget because of the lessons we learned. We blindly chose which hiking trail to go on that day. With a couple bottles of water, a small dog, two children, and my husband and I, we began our hiking adventure. About ten minutes into the hike, we saw a man on horseback leaving the trail and no one else braved the trail that day.

We were focused on the beautiful day ahead of us and had no knowledge about hiking in Arizona and the potential trouble ahead. Our dog was thirsty maybe a third of the way into the hike. We cupped our hands and gave her half of one of the bottles of water. We were all starting to get extremely warm; the heat of the day, the elevation, and little water made things challenging. We had walked too far and there was no turning back. My husband and I were very concerned about the situation in which we had involved our family. We came to a portion of the trail where there had been a forest fire and the trail seemed to end, but thankfully we found the continuing trail.

The sun seemed to get hotter and hotter and all of us were becoming more fatigued and challenged. My husband's hands and feet had swollen, and being concerned, he took off ahead of us to locate the end of this hiking adventure.

He arrived at the car, and he beeped the horn to let us know we were almost there. That sound was music to our ears and gave us the hope we needed to finish the hike.

Without the knowledge of truth, life can be like a dry and parched land where you are wandering around and hoping you'll end up where you should. Traveling through life with little preparation or knowledge of the truth can lead to disastrous consequences. When you don't have the proper provisions, don't know who to follow, when the heat comes, when fires surround you, and when you are without a map, it is a dangerous place in which to wander, as if you are deep in the valley of the shadow of death. **But when you come to the knowledge of the truth, you will have what you need to run your race well and to travel your journey fearing no evil.**

👣 YOUR JOURNEY TO TRUTH

The beginning of my *Called to Truth* journey began years ago when I was listening to a pastor teach on faith. He explained how faith and fear were both in the spiritual realm. Our faith will manifest what we are believing, and fear will manifest what we are fearing. I listened to his teachings on faith over, and over again, but then one day, I no longer needed to hear his teachings on faith. It had penetrated my heart and mind and I understood faith from my spiritual core. This was just the beginning of my journey of truth. Come along on **Your Journey to Truth.**

TRUTH BASIC TRAINING

Before we begin truth basic training, I would like to discuss the process of receiving truth. First, let's look at the purpose of our conscience. Our conscience is a built-in protection created by God for each of us to use to detect right from wrong. When our conscience is clear, our conscience protects us by alerting us to wrong behavior. But on the other hand, if sin has been quite active in our life, it taints our conscience and gradually deteriorates the conscience so it is not detecting right from wrong. For example, if you continue spending a lot of time with people that are influencing you in a negative way, you can begin repeating their bad behavior without any sorrow or recognition about the wrong behavior. Thus, your conscience can be seared over time and eventually it will not alert you to wrong actions like it once did. Second, if your mind has not been renewed by the word of God in certain areas, truth may be difficult to receive in large chunks. Thus, receiving truth in smaller bites may be the best approach as you go through this study. Third, if your heart has not been healed of past hurts, your soul is more likely to listen to the flesh and not to the spirit, which is where truth comes in. All of this is to say, I encourage you to take *Your*

2

Journey to Truth at a pace that allows the truth time to restore your conscience, to renew your mind, and to purify your heart. Be patient with yourself, as you allow God to lead you.

After reading Chapter 1 of *Called to Truth, A Practical, Biblical Guide to Spiritual & Physical Wholeness*, complete the questions below.

1. What is truth and where do I find it?

_____

_____

_____

_____

_____

2. What problems can occur when you follow your own way of thinking?

_____

_____

_____

_____

_____

3. Journal any scripture verses that have specifically impacted your life and were a turning point in your walk with the Lord.

_____

_____

_____

_____

_____

_____

_____

_____

4. Journal any scripture verses you are struggling to understand and are seeking the LORD for revelation.

_____

_____

_____

_____

_____

_____

_____

5. Read Revelation 12:11 and summarize these words. I recommend reading it in the King James Version and two other translations. Write down the definitions of overcome and testimony.

_____

_____

_____

_____

_____

_____

_____

6. What is the good fight of faith? Additional recommended reading: First Timothy 6:6-12.

_____

_____

_____

_____

7. What is freedom through Jesus Christ?

_____

_____

_____

_____

_____

_____

8. Journal the areas in your life where you have found freedom and peace.

_____

_____

_____

_____

_____

_____

_____

9. Journal any area in your life where your freedom, your peace, or your destiny have been stolen? Then spend time in prayer seeking the LORD's guidance in these areas.

_____
_____
_____
_____
_____
_____
_____
_____

⚓ Truth Basic Training Verses

Carefully study the following verses by reading the scripture in various translations including the King James Version. Underline any words that stand out to you, use a *Strong's Concordance*, which is an index of every word in the King James Version, and read the entire chapter of the verse. Journal your notes and summary.

"No man that wars entangle himself with the affairs of this life; that he may please Him who has chosen him to be a soldier." 2 Timothy 2:4

_____
_____
_____
_____
_____
_____
_____

"The LORD is near to all them that call upon Him, to all that call upon Him in truth." Psalm 145:18

_____
_____
_____
_____
_____
_____
_____

"Study to show thyself approved unto God, a workman that need not to be ashamed, rightly dividing the word of truth." 2 Timothy 2:15

Your Journey to Truth

_____

_____

_____

_____

_____

_____

_____

CHAPTER 2

---◆---

MY TRANSFORMATION

The word transform means to change into another form. Likewise, metamorphosis refers to changing form, being transformed, and "change after being with." How are you transformed? The word of God is alive and sharper than any double-edged sword. It penetrates to dividing soul and spirit. When we truly grasp the power in the word of God, we will be amazed at how it changes our inner man by removing darkness from our mind and soul.

Once you have invited Jesus into your life and received Him as your Lord and Savior, the Holy Spirit resides in your spirit, but your mind and soul have not yet been renewed or transformed. Transformation is a process through which the power of the Holy Spirit and the word of God renew our mind and transform our soul.

You are changed by what or who you are closely attached to, by what you are following. If you are living by the ways of the world, there will be signs of who or what you are following in your life. Satan will try to mutate the structure of your spiritual and physical genes. Mutation is "changing of the structure of a gene, resulting in a variant form that may be transmitted to subsequent generations, caused by the alteration of single base units in DNA, or the deletion, insertion, or rearrangement of larger sections of genes or chromosomes." When mutation occurs in our DNA gene, the DNA gene is damaged or changed, altering the message being carried to the gene. When messages are altered, we are being deceived by Satan's mutated messages.

As you meditate, study, speak, believe, and apply the word of God to your life, you are transformed by the truth. If you fall into Satan's devices and plans, you can be mutated by his lies. Years ago, I met up with a friend I hadn't seen in years. I passed right by her at first because her outward appearance was drastically different. She had a beautiful facial feature that was distinctive to her, and it was completely different now. When I saw her that day, she seemed like a different person on the inside and outside. Her outward appearance had changed in almost every way. As we talked, I could hear her pain on the inside and saw her pain on the outside. **Choose today to be transformed by God and cast the cares of this world to God!**

YOUR JOURNEY TO TRUTH

Metamorphosis –

1. After reading Chapter 2 of *Called to Truth, A Practical, Biblical Guide to Spiritual & Physical Wholeness,* and reading the above introduction to this chapter, journal your understanding of the metamorphosis process. Journal how the word of God plays a major part in the metamorphosis process of the believer.

_____

_____

_____

_____

_____

_____

_____

2. If you have attached yourself to sin, hurt, and the world's ways, how can this mutate or alter a person?

_____

_____

_____

_____

_____

_____

_____

_____

3. According to Second Corinthians 5:17, *"Therefore if any man be in Christ, he is a new creature; old things are passed away; behold, all things are become new."* After reading Chapter 2, you have had an opportunity to hear My Transformation.

Being a new creation in Christ, you will be able to identify the old things that are passed away and the new creation you are in Christ. Journal what it means for you to be a "new creation" in Christ.

_____
_____
_____
_____
_____
_____
_____
_____

4. What are the signs or evidence of a transformation in you?

_____
_____
_____
_____
_____
_____
_____
_____
_____

5. Journal your relationship with Jesus. If you have not accepted Jesus as your Lord and Savior, but you want to know more about the Lord, pray and ask Him to reveal Himself to you. Journal any questions you want to ask Jesus.

_____
_____
_____
_____
_____
_____
_____
_____
_____
_____

6. Whether you are a new believer or have been a believer for a long time, journal your testimony and how the LORD has transformed your life thus far. Ask the LORD to bring to remembrance all He has done for you, how He has renewed your mind, and how He has purified your heart. List the evidence in your life that you no longer follow the world's ways. Journal the evidence that you are not a world follower but a Christ follower. This process is about testing yourself and where you are in your spiritual walk. According to Second Corinthians 3:18, you are being transformed into His image from glory to glory, therefore, it is a process that continues throughout your lifetime.

MY TRANSFORMATION TESTIMONY:

_____
_____
_____
_____
_____
_____
_____
_____
_____
_____
_____
_____
_____
_____
_____
_____
_____
_____
_____
_____
_____
_____
_____
_____
_____
_____

7. According to Psalm 139:23-24, "*Search me, O God, and know my heart: try me, and know my thoughts: and see if there be any wicked way in me, and lead me in the way everlasting.*" Journal any area in your life you want and need to overcome. What obstacles are in your life? Where does the enemy have a foothold on your destiny? Where are you overwhelmed in your life?

I WANT TO OVERCOME THESE OBSTABLES IN MY LIFE AND NEED YOUR HELP HEAVENLY FATHER:

_____

_____

_____

_____

_____

_____

_____

_____

_____

_____

_____

_____

_____

_____

_____

_____

_____

_____

_____

_____

_____

_____

_____

⚓ Truth Basic Training Verses

Carefully study the following verses by reading the scripture in various translations, including the King James Version; underline any words that stand out to you; use a *Strong's Concordance* which is an index of every word in the King James Version, and read the entire chapter of the verse. Journal your notes and summary.

"And be not conformed to this world: but be you transformed by the renewing of your mind, that you may prove what is that good, and acceptable, and perfect, will of God." Romans 12:2

_____

_____

_____

_____

_____

_____

"But we all, with open face beholding as in a glass the glory of the Lord, are changed into the same image from glory to glory, even as by the Spirit of the Lord." 2 Corinthians 3:18

_____

_____

_____

_____

_____

_____

CHAPTER 3

---✣---

SHINING THE LIGHT ON LIES

It may not seem exciting or pleasant to look in the mirror to examine what your mind and soul are reflecting, but on the other hand, it may represent a breakthrough and a freedom richer than gold. The word of God shines the light on your mind and soul. It will guide you to recognize the lies and sin that are holding you back from the fullness of the LORD.

Lies come into our life very subtly. The thief comes to steal, kill, and destroy. A thief who has mastered the art of stealing is cunning and knows how to find access into our lives without being noticed. Satan can steal our identity in Christ by convincing us to follow him instead of God. Satan's ways have not changed since the Garden of Eden where Adam and Eve fell into his trap. Satan was even conniving enough to try and tempt Jesus in the desert.

Satan's ways have not changed but he does change his tactics to lure each of us differently, depending on our backgrounds, experiences, and personalities. The demonic realm will follow us and monitor us to discover what lies we are most likely to believe; it will search for areas of our life where we have left the door open for evil to enter. The thief looks for easy access. What evil do you need to shut down, end or close in your life? Come along on **Your Journey to Truth** to shut down evil in your life.

YOUR JOURNEY TO TRUTH

EXPOSE THE LIES OR THEY WILL GROW

1. After reading Chapter 3 of *Called to Truth, A Practical, Biblical Guide to Spiritual & Physical Wholeness*, you will notice that the biggest lie I believed in

my life was fear and how I was serving fear by following it. According to Second Corinthians 2:11, you are not to be ignorant of Satan's devices lest he get an advantage in your life. You don't want Satan to gain a foothold in your mind, your heart, or your free will. Please review pages 8-9 of *Called to Truth, A Practical, Biblical Guide to Spiritual & Physical Wholeness,* where I have listed <u>eleven ways deceptions and lies can come into your life</u>. After you have reviewed these, journal below a summary of these points and any revelations you have after reviewing this list.

We will look at Elvis Presley's life and how it displays the spiritual battle for our souls. The spiritual battle was very real in Elvis Presley's life. As Elvis searched for meaning in his life, at times he was led down the wrong road. Elvis Presley had someone in his life who influenced him towards other religions and spiritual practices that were not biblical and took him down a dark and dangerous road. In addition to Christianity, Elvis studied Hinduism, numerology, positive thinking, new-age, meditation, and theosophy. His interest in these other spiritual practices was troublesome to those who were in Elvis's life who also loved Jesus. We may think if we dabble in other spiritual practices, it won't affect us, but the truth is, when evil tries to gain ground in our life it is usually a gradual process of slowly destroying the spiritual nerve-endings of our conscience. Additionally, Elvis' experimentation with drugs affected his ability to make wise decisions. The world was fighting for Elvis' heart and attention. God had a plan for Elvis' life and the battle raged for who would get his attention.

In 1976, Rex Humbard and his wife Maude Aimee met with Elvis privately. Maude Aimee told Elvis she had prayed for years that he would become a bell sheep for God. She explained that in Israel they put a bell on one sheep and all the other sheep would follow. Maude Aimee said to Elvis, *"If you fully dedicated your life to God, you could lead millions of people into the kingdom of the Lord."*

Elvis was brought up to know the Lord but as fame came into his life so did many temptations. The people in Elvis's life that cared about him said he never rejected his faith in Jesus Christ, even though he stumbled. There was a tug of war for his soul and destiny. Rick Stanley, Elvis' stepbrother, was with Elvis on the night of his death and heard Elvis pray to the Lord for His help. A day earlier Rick heard Elvis pray for forgiveness.

The spiritual battle is very real, and Elvis was no different than us in that regard. Lessons we can learn include: a) be watchful of who is in your inner circle of friends and advisors; b) be watchful to what you open the door and come into agreement with that is not of God; c) our destiny is in Christ not the world; d) the battle for our souls is real, and we need to be vigilant; e) now is the time to live fully for the LORD, f) and never give up the good fight of faith!

2. Below are some statements to test and determine if evil has gained access in your life. This process is meant to help you evaluate your life, thereby revealing where lies have crept in. We are all responsible for our own life and our behavior. Listed are some questions to test your heart, mind, and choices. Place a checkmark next to the points that need to be examined for correction. (Note: if you are following and obeying the Holy Spirit, this step is probably not necessary. But if you are struggling to break free, these questions can assist you.)

SHINING THE LIGHT ON YOUR HEART, YOUR MIND, AND YOUR CHOICES

Practicing to sin (habitual)

____I recognize I am sinning but continue to sin anyway without seeking God's help or repenting.

____I break the spiritual laws and commandments of God with no repentance or prayer.

____I keep secret sins that only I know about, but for which I neither repent nor ask God's help.

____The Holy Spirit has been leading me to change an area of my life, but I keep ignoring His guidance and do not repent (a change of mind).

Lacking intimate relationship with the LORD

____I do not study the word of God myself but only listen to what others teach me about God.

____I ignore parts of the Bible that make me feel uncomfortable and that I do not agree with.

____I talk about my problems frequently, and I have not learned to release my cares to God.

Problems with forgiving yourself or forgiving others

_____I have a hard time forgiving people.

_____I get angry or hurt by my family members every time I am with them.

_____I am not able to forgive myself. I live with shame, guilt, or regret.

_____I get offended regularly. I take offense (receive the offense) and don't cast it off.

_____I have resentment, bitterness, or unforgiveness towards another person.

_____Family and friends who love me are trying to help me with wise counsel, but I take offense and don't use their feedback.

Idolatry

_____I love money or possessions more than God; my actions reveal this.

_____I love my status; my identity is found in my status.

_____I love my children, spouse, or another person more than God; my actions reveal this.

_____I love my life more than God; my actions reveal I put myself above God.

Spiritual oppression

_____Every time I try to read the Bible, I fall asleep.

_____When I listen to a biblical teaching, I feel sick to my stomach or get a headache.

_____My thoughts are racing and out of control.

_____Knowingly or unknowingly, I am not resisting Satan, and I have given up my authority to kick Satan out of my life.

_____I am miserable most of the time.

_____I frequently get offended.

_____I feel like I am carrying around extra baggage that I can't get rid of.

_____I keep repeating bad behavior that I despise.

Following man-made rules instead of faith in Jesus Christ

_____I follow man-made rules and traditions that were handed down through generations but are not based on biblical truth. I expect myself and others to live by these traditions because they are familiar and comfortable to me.

_____I diligently follow man-made rules in the church, and they are as important to me as the scripture; my actions reveal this.

_____The only time I spend with God is when I am at church on Sunday. My relationship with Jesus is on Sunday only.

Occult activity

_____I engage in occult activity: reading my horoscope, magic, idol statutes in my possession, witchcraft or sorcery role playing games, manipulation, rebellion, superstition, charms, yoga, Ouija boards, talking to the dead, Wicca, Reiki, and many others. An occult activity is seeking a supernatural power for enlightenment or protection that is not from God.

Witchcraft

_____I manipulate others to get my way by coercing them, smooth talking, etc.

_____I use ulterior motives to manipulate someone's free will.

Stolen identity

_____I don't usually share the truth; I tend to tell people what they want to hear.

_____I have character traits that I am holding onto, but that God wants to remove.

_____I am known as a liar by people who know me.

_____I often commit to things to which I don't follow through. My word can't be trusted.

_____I put more of my time and energy into my outward image than what is going on internally (my mind and heart).

_____I am not authentic with people. I am insincere and fake with people.

Talebearer (gossip)/prideful/accusatory

_____I cut people down with my words. If I am honest with myself, this makes me feel better about myself.

_____I act like I really care about someone when they are in front of me. When they leave, I start talking about all their faults and make accusations about them.

_____I maliciously reveal secrets about people.

Unloving towards self

_____I do not like or love myself.

_____I compare myself with others and believe that others are better than me.

Passivity

_____I don't cast off evil thoughts and imaginations.

_____People have said mean and hurtful things about me, and I just accept their words and believe them.

_____I have become lazy in my walk with the Lord. I am not seeking God.

_____I feel like I have no choices in my life. My life is moving in a direction that I don't want it to go, and I let it happen.

_____I often tell others my problems but don't want help.

_____ I don't want to change my behavior.

Living under a curse

_____I do not honor my mother or father.

_____I have dishonored by parents and never repented.

_____I had word curses spoken over me that were never renounced.

Selfishness

_____I am only concerned about myself; I do not have time to help anyone else.

_____The evidence in my life shows that I am only concerned with my life and my issues and anxieties, I can't even remember the last time I helped anyone else.

Envy and Jealousy

_____I feel envy and jealousy when I am around my friends or family.

_____I feel anger rising in my heart when others get things that I am waiting for.

Discontentment/Ungrateful

_____Others tell me I complain a lot.

_____I am never content with what I have.

_____I have a hard time recognizing the blessings in my life.

Careless with words/speaking idle words/speaking death

_____I curse people with my words.

_____I don't speak words of life but words of death over myself and others.

_____I use my words carelessly and speak idle words without thought.

_____I speak hurtful words to others and continue this pattern with no repentance.

Fearful

_____I make decisions out of fear which reveals I am not trusting God.

_____I recognize that I am fearful in situations where I should not be.

_____Fear affects my daily activities.

Pride

_____I am often defensive.

_____I frequently have difficulty getting along with people.

_____I take offense anytime someone gives me corrective feedback.

_____I never make a mistake; it is always someone else's mistake.

After examination and reflection on the above examples, journal what has been highlighted to you. Spend time in prayer with what has been revealed to you.

_____
_____
_____
_____
_____
_____

_____
_____
_____
_____
_____
_____
_____
_____
_____
_____
_____
_____
_____
_____
_____
_____
_____
_____

⚓ Truth Basic Training Verses

Carefully study the following verses by reading the scripture in various translations, including the King James Version. Underline any words that stand out to you; use a *Strong's Concordance*, which is an index of every word in the King James Version, and read the entire chapter of the verse. Journal your notes and summary.

"And have no fellowship with the unfruitful works of darkness, but rather reprove (expose) them." Ephesians 5:11

_____
_____
_____

"For the wisdom of this world is foolishness with God. For it is written, He taketh the wise in their own craftiness." 1 Corinthians 3:19

_____
_____
_____

CHAPTER 4

BATTLE PLAN

A battle plan for war will include the following: proper communication between the operations and commanders; preparation of weapons and equipment; strategic planning; training of armed forces; studying the tactics of the enemy, and the deployment of the armed forces. The battle plan for the soldier of Jesus Christ will include the following: communication and a strong relationship with the Commander (God); studying and preparing with the word of God; prayer strategies; being trained up in the truths of Jesus Christ; knowing the tactics of the enemy (Satan), and moving into action by putting on the whole armor of God.

As I thought about what example would best display our spiritual battles as believers, I thought about the soldier who saved 75 lives in the battle at Hacksaw Ridge. A soldier, Desmond Doss, was a combat medic in World War II in Okinawa. Desmond Doss vowed not to kill and would not touch a weapon. Doss was a believer in the Lord Jesus Christ, a fact that was known among the other soldiers who would throw shoes at him while he prayed. Then in 1945, Doss' company climbed Hacksaw Ridge where the enemy soldiers were waiting. While the battle at Hacksaw Ridge was raging with gunfire and explosives, Doss was pulling wounded soldiers to the edge of the ridge and tying them to a rope to lower wounded soldiers to the other medics below. Doss said, *"I was praying the whole time. I just kept praying, 'Lord, please help me get one more."* Over a twelve-hour span, Doss saved 75 men without any gun or weapon other than prayer.

As the spiritual battle rages for people's souls, our prayers bring life where there was death. Our prayers bring truth where there were lies. Our prayers open opportunities for people to hear the truth of Jesus Christ. With our prayers, what we bind (fasten, prohibit, forbid) on earth will be bound in heaven, and what we loose (unbind, set free) on earth will be loosed in heaven. Our prayers are like arrows and swords fighting the evil spiritual realm. **Prepare your battle plan to defeat evil in your life!**

👣 YOUR JOURNEY TO TRUTH

THE FOLLOWERS OF JESUS CHRIST DO NOT WAGE WAR AS THE WORLD DOES

1. After reading Chapter 4 of *Called to Truth, A Practical, Biblical Guide to Spiritual & Physical Wholeness*, what is a spiritual Battle Plan?

_____
_____
_____
_____
_____
_____
_____

Before answering the questions below and creating your Battle Plan, I recommend reading the entire book of *Called to Truth, A Practical, Biblical Guide to Spiritual & Physical Wholeness*.

2. What preventive measures will I take in my spiritual life to purposefully guard my life from evil, sin, and the lies of Satan?

_____
_____
_____
_____
_____
_____
_____

3. Give examples of God's order (read pages 16-17 of Chapter 5 from *Called to Truth, A Practical, Biblical Guide to Spiritual & Physical Wholeness*).

_____
_____
_____
_____
_____

_____
_____

Am I resisting the order of God and if so, in what areas?

_____
_____
_____
_____
_____
_____
_____
_____

Journal your Battle Plan to follow God's order in your life.

_____
_____
_____
_____
_____
_____
_____
_____

4. Am I living a life of forgiveness? (Refer to page 22 and 29 of *Called to Truth, A Practical, Biblical Guide to Spiritual & Physical Wholeness*.) If not, what are the steps I will take to live a life of forgiving myself and others?

_____
_____
_____
_____
_____
_____
_____
_____
_____

5. Do I have a personal relationship with Jesus Christ during the week with prayer and studying the word of God? If not, what are the steps I will take to get my spiritual house in order?

_____
_____
_____
_____
_____
_____
_____
_____
_____

6. Do I live a life focused on my relationship with the LORD? Is my life so busy I only think about worldly concerns and schedules? What changes will I make for myself to refocus my life on the LORD and His plans for me? Journal your vision and Battle Plan for yourself and commit them to the LORD.

_____
_____
_____
_____
_____
_____
_____
_____
_____
_____

7. Am I walking in doubt or unbelief? What steps will I take to exercise my faith muscle and rebuke doubt and unbelief? (Refer to Chapter 9 of *Called to Truth, A Practical, Biblical Guide to Spiritual & Physical Wholeness.*)

_____
_____
_____
_____
_____
_____
_____

8. Do I have a strong prayer life? Do I pray spiritual warfare prayers? Do I pray together with my spouse? Do I pray with my family? Do I pray with other believers? (Refer to Chapter 8 of *Called to Truth, A Practical, Biblical Guide to Spiritual & Physical Wholeness.*) Journal your Battle Plan for your prayer life.

_____
_____
_____
_____
_____
_____
_____
_____

9. Do I use my mouth for speaking truth and love or for speaking lies and evil? Am I a mouthpiece for God or a mouthpiece for Satan? What plans will I put in place to increase the words of life I speak and renounce any unprofitable words that come out of my mouth? (Refer to pages 76-78, and 94 of "_Called to Truth, A Practical, Biblical Guide to Spiritual & Physical Wholeness._")

_____
_____
_____
_____
_____
_____
_____

10. Are my activities pleasing to God or am I living like the world? (Refer to Chapter 17 of _Called to Truth, A Practical, Biblical Guide to Spiritual & Physical Wholeness._) Journal your Battle Plan to live a life pleasing to God.

_____
_____
_____
_____
_____
_____
_____
_____

11. Am I serving others or just myself?

_____
_____
_____

_____
_____
_____
_____

Journal your Battle Plan to serve God and others.

_____
_____
_____
_____
_____
_____
_____

12. Am I living for my own enjoyment and not asking the LORD what He wants me to do with my life?

_____
_____
_____
_____
_____
_____
_____

Journal your Battle Plan to walk out the plans God has for your life.

_____
_____
_____
_____
_____
_____
_____

13. Recognizing problem areas in your life

Am I engaging in occult activities (any practice that tries to gain supernatural power, abilities, or knowledge apart from God)?

_____
_____
_____
_____

_____
_____
_____

Is idolatry in my life (worship by showing reverence and adoration to someone or something other than God)?

_____
_____
_____
_____
_____
_____
_____
_____

<u>Circle the areas that are problem areas in your life:</u>

Do I live a life of hatred or unforgiveness,

gossip

activities that are producing bad fruit

addictions, obsessions, compulsions

cursing others or myself

hurting myself or others

manipulating others

living in fear

living an unintentional life

living a lukewarm life

living solely for my own comfort and enjoyment

not resisting Satan, etc.? (Refer to Chapter 6 of _Called to Truth, A Practical, Biblical Guide to Spiritual & Physical Wholeness._)

Now journal your strategic Battle Plan to renounce the areas you have recognized as problem areas in your life. <u>Once you have completed the remaining chapters of this study guide, you will be more equipped to complete this Battle Plan.</u>

_____
_____
_____
_____
_____
_____
_____
_____
_____
_____
_____
_____

⚓ Truth Basic Training Verses

Carefully study the following verses by reading the scripture in various translations, including the King James Version. Underline any words that stand out to you, use a *Strong's Concordance* which is an index of every word in the King James Version, and read the entire chapter of the verse. Journal your notes and summary.

"For though we walk in the flesh, we do not war after the flesh. For the weapons of our warfare are not carnal, but mighty through God to the pulling down of strongholds. Casting down imaginations, and every high thing that exalts itself against the knowledge of God, and bringing into captivity every thought to the obedience of Christ." Second Corinthians 10:3-5

_____
_____
_____
_____
_____
_____
_____
_____
_____
_____

CHAPTER 5

---•❧•---

THE AUTHOR OF ORDER

Our Heavenly Father, the Creator of all, made His creation with spiritual laws and principles that operate the spiritual and physical realm. God's creation was made with an order to its design. God's design or blueprint was not made haphazardly. To understand the blueprint of creation, you need to know the Creator of the Universe.

The word of God says a curse without a cause does not happen; scripture says we reap what we sow. God's spiritual principles were set in place to create order within His creation. The LORD's spiritual laws and principles are throughout the Bible, and they are blessings when the conditions are met.

This chapter will help you understand the order in God's creation. The more you study the spiritual principles of the Bible, the more understanding you will have of how God's universe operates. For example, scripture says, *"the fear of the LORD is the beginning of knowledge."* If you have no understanding of the fear of the LORD, how will you have knowledge of who God is and His spiritual principles? Let's dive into **Your Journey to Truth** for revelation.

👣 YOUR JOURNEY TO TRUTH

Before we begin with the questions below, I want to share with you a revelation I had that may help you understand God's order. In my younger years especially, I used to have an opinion about issues. But what I realized as God revealed His truths to me was that my opinion was of very little value, especially if it went against God's order. I first needed to understand The Author of Order and how God created the world to operate. His creation has spiritual principles and laws they operate under. If I am thinking that I need to come up with my opinions about issues in the world without consulting what God's word says, I will be in trouble. When I am looking at the worldly evidence of something and coming up with my opinions, the flaws of my human views and worldly evidence will give me a false conclusion. Man's opinions are ever-changing, and God's ways never go against His divine order. In my twenties, I thought it was part of my critical college thinking to determine where I stood on issues. The problem was, I didn't understand, at that point in my life, that God has an order to His creation, a spiritual order to how things operate. God's redeeming power changes things and His ways are not our ways. As I have grown in the knowledge of the LORD, it is from the fear of the LORD and understanding His truths that all things are possible. Man's ways or opinions are ever-changing; as human beings we only have a small amount of knowledge compared to our Creator. Therefore, we should be searching God's word for all our questions, not the view of men which leads to destruction. We are to follow and obey God's spiritual principles by fearing the LORD, repenting, forgiveness, etc. We are not to look back at the world's ways like Lot's wife did as she left Sodom and Gomorrah and turned into a pillar of salt. Don't regret not following the world's ways or feeling the need to hear everyone's opinions about issues that God has already spoken on. Seek His truths and follow that. Don't look back at the Sodom and Gomorrah of the world and its deceptive opinions, but run to the LORD. *"The name of the LORD is a strong tower; the righteous runs into it, and is safe."* Proverbs 18:10.

HAVE I NOT COMMANDED YOU?

1. After reading chapter 5 of *Called to Truth, A Practical, Biblical Guide to Spiritual & Physical Wholeness*, journal examples of God's order in His creation.

_____

_____

_____

_____

_____

_____

_____

_____

_____

_____

2. According to chapter 5, journal examples of disorder manifesting on the earth.

---

3. Give examples in your own life where you have stepped out of God's protective order.

---

4. What is God's order for the family? (Refer to page 17 of *Called to Truth, A Practical, Biblical Guide to Spiritual & Physical Wholeness*.) Is your family in order according to the word of God? If not, where does order need to be restored? When you step out of God's order, you step out of His protection. For example: when a house is divided against itself, it cannot stand. Journal examples of order within your family and then examples of anything that is out of order.

---

5. After reviewing page 15, OUR RELATIONSHIP WITH GOD, and page 18, FEAR OF GOD from *Called to Truth, A Practical, Biblical Guide to Spiritual & Physical Wholeness*, answer the following questions:

Your Journey to Truth

Am I intentional about the time I spend with God?

_____
_____
_____
_____

Do I honor God with my time, treasure, and talent?

_____
_____
_____
_____

What is the fear of the LORD?

_____
_____
_____
_____

Do I have the fear of the LORD?

_____
_____
_____
_____
_____

Do I talk to God about my struggles and ask for His strength and guidance?

_____
_____
_____
_____
_____
_____
_____

Do I earnestly seek His truth (the word of God) above all?

_____
_____
_____
_____

Are there any warning signs in my life that I have put other people or things above God, or even at the same level as God?

_____
_____
_____
_____
_____

Do I love not my life according to Revelation 12:11?

_____
_____
_____
_____

6. According to page 17 on GOD'S AUTHORITY, who are God's workers on earth, and what characteristics reveal who they are? Who is bringing heaven to earth?

_____
_____
_____
_____
_____

7. How do you know the will of God (refer to page 18)?

_____
_____
_____
_____
_____
_____

8. Journal in your own words what it means to be born again (refer to page 19-20 of _Called to Truth, A Practical, Biblical Guide to Spiritual & Physical Wholeness_).

_____
_____
_____
_____
_____

_____
_____

9. Journal what it means to confess Christ as your Lord and Savior.

_____
_____
_____
_____
_____

10. Journal what it means to be drawn and led by the Holy Spirit.

_____
_____
_____
_____

11. Journal what it means to be drawn to repentance and baptized.

_____
_____
_____
_____
_____

12. Journal what it means to have godly sorrow which leads to repentance and salvation.

_____
_____
_____
_____
_____

13. Describe sanctification.

_____
_____
_____
_____
_____

14. What is the purpose of trials and temptations?

_____
_____
_____
_____
_____

15. What is revealed by the way you handle trials and temptations?

_____
_____
_____
_____
_____

16. What is repentance, and what does God say about repentance?

_____
_____
_____
_____
_____

17. Define forgiveness, and who are you to forgive?

_____
_____
_____
_____
_____

18. How does your obedience to God and having a forgiving heart bless you?

_____
_____
_____
_____

19. Describe the characteristics of someone who is obedient to God.

_____
_____
_____
_____
_____

20. After reading pages 23-24, SIN AND DISOBEDIENCE from _Called to Truth, A Practical, Biblical Guide to Spiritual & Physical Wholeness_, what are the

ways to remain under the blessing of obedience rather than the curse of disobedience and sin?

_____

_____

_____

_____

_____

_____

21. According to Psalm 103 and PERSONAL TESTIMONY on pages 24-25 of *Called to Truth, A Practical, Biblical Guide to Spiritual & Physical Wholeness*, answer the following questions:

Define iniquity.

_____

_____

What iniquities does God forgive?

_____

_____

What diseases does God heal?

_____

_____

What benefits does He not want us to forget?

_____

_____

List the benefits in Psalm 103.

_____

_____

_____

_____

_____

_____

After reading all of Psalm 103, review verses 11, 13, and 17. Who does the LORD have mercy on?

_____

⚓ Truth Basic Training Verses

Carefully study the following verses by reading the scripture in various translations, including the King James Version. Underline any words that stand out to you. Use a *Strong's Concordance*, which is an index of every word in the King James Version, and read the entire chapter of the verse. Journal your notes and summary.

"Have not I commanded you? Be strong and of a good courage; be not afraid, neither be you dismayed: for the LORD your God is with you wherever you go." Joshua 1:9

_____

_____

_____

_____

_____

_____

_____

_____

CHAPTER 6

---◆---

OUR OBEDIENCE

With obedience, you have to make a choice: Who will you serve? Who has your heart? Whoever has your heart is who you will be obeying. Noah walked with God and served God in obedience. Noah built the ark with precise instructions. The instructions for us today are in the word of God. At the time of Noah, there was great wickedness and only evil imagination in man's heart. Noah followed God's instructions, and it kept Noah and his family safe. Let's begin **Your Journey to Truth** on God's divine order of our obedience.

🐾 YOUR JOURNEY TO TRUTH

If a father does not have a relationship with his children and he tries to enforce his rules in the house, it is quite possible the children will rebel. But when the father of the house has a relationship with his children, his children will most likely obey his rules because they love their father and want to please him. The same applies to our Heavenly Father. If we have a relationship with our Heavenly Father, we want to please Him and want to obey His voice, His commandments, and His spiritual laws because we know He loves us and wants what is best for us. We come to God the Father through our relationship with Jesus Christ.

1. Do you have a personal relationship with your Heavenly Father? If not, that is the essential first step to following Him in obedience. According to John 14:6, Jesus said unto him, *"I am the way, the truth, and the life: no man cometh unto the Father, but by me."* We have a relationship with our Heavenly Father through our faith in Jesus Christ as our Lord and Savior. Your Heavenly

Father reached down from heaven with His love for you and sent His love (His Son, Jesus) to pay the price for your sins. According to John 15:4, "*Abide in Me, and I in you. As the branch cannot bear fruit of itself, unless it abides in the vine, neither can you, unless you abide in Me.*" Through your faith in Jesus Christ as your Lord and Savior, God wants to have a personal relationship with you as His son or daughter. **Write a letter to God telling Him your thoughts and sharing what is on your heart.**

_____

_____

_____

_____

_____

2. After reading Chapter 6 of *Called to Truth, A Practical, Biblical Guide to Spiritual & Physical Wholeness*, what are the characteristics of a Pharisee? According to the verses listed on page 27, how should all believers be examining themselves?

_____

_____

_____

_____

_____

_____

_____

_____

_____

3. Let's examine the statement listed on page 27 of *Called to Truth, A Practical, Biblical Guide to Spiritual & Physical Wholeness*: "…the traditions of men became the commandments the Pharisees lived by." To explore this statement, we will look at a few references from Mark 7, amplified version: *"there are many other things (oral, man-made laws and traditions handed down to them) which they follow diligently," "why do Your disciples not live their lives according to the tradition of the elders?" "you disregard and neglect the commandment of God, and cling (faithfully) to the tradition of men," "so you nullify the (authority of the) word of God (acting as if it did not apply) because of your tradition which you have handed down (through the elders)."* What are some of the traditions (man-made rules) that you may be following that can cause you to fall into the trap of a religious Pharisee? (To assist you in answering this question, you can study Mark 7 and examine the rules you live by to test whether they are of God or man-made. Another valuable test is to examine the amount of time and effort you put into learning the word of God and following God's principles versus any man-made rules or traditions.)

_____

_____

_____

_____

_____

_____

_____

_____

_____

_____

_____

_____

_____

_____

_____

_____

_____

4. What does it mean to practice sinning?

_____

_____

_____

5. From page 28 of _Called to Truth, A Practical, Biblical Guide to Spiritual &_ _Physical Wholeness_, what is the Bible referring to specifically when it talks about the heart?

_____

_____

_____

_____

_____

_____

_____

6. After reading Matthew 15:18, summarize this verse in your own words.

_____

_____

_____

_____

7. Where is your treasure according to page 28?

_____

_____

_____

_____

8. Journal what it means to be careful and not to put a stumbling block in another person's way? Give an example. (See page 28.)

_____

_____

_____

_____

_____

_____
_____
_____
_____
_____

9. How do you describe forgiveness according to page 29? How do you know if you have forgiven someone?

_____
_____
_____
_____
_____
_____
_____
_____
_____

10. What harm does unforgiveness have on the body, according to page 30?

_____
_____
_____
_____
_____
_____
_____

11. As a follower of Jesus Christ, you are not to let the sun go down holding anger, bitterness, or unforgiveness in your heart. The longer you have held onto these ill feelings in your heart, the more damage it can do to you.

Is there someone you have not forgiven? Is there someone you are holding hostage in your soul? Is there someone from whom you have received (taken) an offense and are holding onto this person in your soul? Do you still have bitterness over something that happened many years ago? Do you still have ill feelings towards someone you thought you forgave?

Signs you may be holding unforgiveness in your heart:

a) having feelings of anger in your heart about the situation that occurred, and the person involved; or

b) having feelings of resentment towards that person; or

c) holding bitterness in your heart; or

d) hearing that person's name brings up ill feelings in your heart; or

e) you have decided that this person is indebted to you; or

f) rehearsing the story over and over that caused you pain and never letting it go, or

g) bad thoughts enter your mind about the person that caused you pain or may even be deflected to another person, and you don't cast off these thoughts.

Forgiving someone is not saying you must trust them again or that what they did was right; you are releasing the person to God because God is the Judge. We are not to hold anger or ill feelings towards others; we are to release the situation to God for Him to handle. When we don't forgive, we are putting ourselves in bondage. We are not free until we release the person to God and forgive from our heart.

When you have made the decision to release the person to God and forgive them, release the person out of your belly (out of your soul). Release the past situation and person to the LORD and receive the LORD's healing love. Journal your prayer of releasing the pain to God and receiving His love.

_____
_____
_____
_____
_____
_____
_____
_____
_____
_____
_____
_____
_____

12. What is repentance according to page 30, and why is it necessary?

_____
_____
_____
_____
_____

13. If you say you have not sinned, what does God say about you?

_____

_____

14. An iniquity is an evil purpose or desire in the heart and is a heart issue. Sin is the acting out of the sinful purpose or desire. Define the difference between sin, transgression, and iniquity according to pages 30-31.

_____

_____

_____

_____

_____

_____

_____

_____

15. Let's read and review Psalm 51 from page 31 of *Called to Truth, A Practical, Biblical Guide to Spiritual & Physical Wholeness*. In verse 6 of Psalm 51, God desires truth in our inward parts and makes us to know wisdom. What benefits do truth and wisdom have to our inward parts?

_____

_____

_____

_____

_____

_____

_____

_____

⚓ Truth Basic Training Verses

Carefully study the following verses by reading the scripture in various translations, including the King James Version; underline any words that stand out to you; use a Strong's Concordance which is an index of every word in the King James Version, and read the entire chapter of the verse. Journal your notes and summary.

"You were running the race well; who has interfered and prevented you from obeying the truth? This (deception) persuasion is not from Him who called you to freedom in Christ."
Galatians 5:7 Amplified

———————————————————————————
———————————————————————————
———————————————————————————
———————————————————————————
———————————————————————————
———————————————————————————

"He who covers his sin will not prosper, but whoever confesses and forsakes them will have mercy." Proverbs 28:13

———————————————————————————
———————————————————————————
———————————————————————————
———————————————————————————
———————————————————————————

"Poverty and shame shall be to him that refuses instruction: but he that regards reproof shall be honored." Proverbs 13:18

———————————————————————————
———————————————————————————
———————————————————————————
———————————————————————————
———————————————————————————

CHAPTER 7

TRUE IDENTITY OR STOLEN IDENTITY

God has made you unique, like no one else on the earth. You were created with a purpose and a plan for your life. The world will tell you that you need to fit into this or that group of people, but God made you special. God loves you the way He created you. Satan will try to:

- Tell you that you are not a boy or not a girl but something in between;

- Tell you that there is no purpose for your life;

- Entice you to do evil and lie to get things you want;

- Tell you that you aren't special and that you were a mistake;

- Use the problems that have happened in your life to make you feel like you are no good;

- Speak lies to you that you should hate yourself and others;

- Tell you that you are so messed up that God can't use you anymore;

- Tell you that you are unlovable, and/or

- Tell you that you must lie and cheat to make a way in this world.

But guess what? Satan is the father of lies. Satan has lied to you because that is who he is, but that is not who you are! Come along on **Your Journey to Truth** and take your rightful place in God's kingdom as a son or daughter of the King!

👣 YOUR JOURNEY TO TRUTH

1. After reading Chapter 7 of Called to Truth, *A Practical, Biblical Guide to Spiritual & Physical Wholeness*, what are the various signs that someone is walking in their True identity?

_____

_____

_____

_____

_____

_____

_____

_____

2. Are you authentic or are you masquerading through life pretending you are someone you are not, being what others say you are, or letting the world define you?

_____

_____

_____

_____

Are you hiding who God created you to be and masquerading as someone that is acceptable to the world?

_____

_____

_____

_____

_____

Have you believed a lie about who you are?

_____

_____

_____

_____

What are signs someone is walking in a stolen identity?

_____
_____
_____
_____
_____

3. Are you acting differently on Monday morning than you are on Friday night? Are you acting differently on Sunday morning then you are on Saturday night?

_____
_____
_____
_____
_____

Is your character different depending on who you are with?

_____
_____
_____
_____
_____

Are you putting on a performance to be accepted? Journal your thoughts.

_____
_____
_____
_____
_____
_____
_____

4. Do you know what God says about His children? According to the Word of God, as believers in Jesus Christ, you are no longer a servant but an heir of God. You no longer serve sin but are sons and daughters of the King (Galatians 4:7, 2 Corinthians 6:18, Ephesians 2:6). When you look in the mirror of your inner man (your heart, your mind, and your spirit), do you believe what God says about your identity or do you believe in the plans that the world and Satan have for you?

_____
_____
_____

_____
_____
_____
_____
_____
_____
_____

What do you believe about yourself? Journal what you believe about yourself and access whether it aligns with what God says about His plans for you according to Psalm 139:13-18 and Jeremiah 29:11-13.

_____
_____
_____
_____
_____
_____
_____
_____
_____
_____

5. Let's examine a statement made on page 32 of _Called to Truth, A Practical, Biblical Guide to Spiritual & Physical Wholeness_: "what you agree with is really important, because an agreement with lies will lead to a stolen identity; an agreement with the truth about who God made you to be will lead you to your true identity." Give examples of how believing a lie can lead to a stolen identity and how believing the truth can lead to walking out your destiny.

_____
_____
_____
_____
_____
_____
_____
_____
_____
_____

6. Now it is time to renounce any lies you have believed about your identity. Renouncing means to forbid, refuse, and disown. Journal your declaration of renouncing any lies you once believed about your identity.

_____
_____
_____
_____
_____
_____
_____
_____
_____
_____
_____
_____
_____
_____

7. Journal life affirming statements about your life, about how God created you, and about your future. In your life affirming statements, include scriptures and include your name in the scripture. Examples of scriptures you may want to use: Psalm 139; Jeremiah 29:11; Psalm 23; Psalm 103:1-6; Galatians 4:7, and 2 Corinthians 6:18. When you have completed journaling your life affirming statements, decree and declare out loud your TRUE IDENTITY. You should read your life affirming statements over and over until you believe them in your heart.

_____
_____
_____
_____
_____
_____
_____
_____
_____
_____
_____
_____

_____
_____
_____
_____
_____
_____
_____
_____
_____
_____
_____
_____
_____
_____
_____
_____
_____

8. How do you protect your identity according to page 34 of *Called to Truth, A Practical, Biblical Guide to Spiritual & Physical Wholeness?* Journal the ways to safeguard your True Identity in Christ.

_____
_____
_____
_____
_____
_____
_____
_____
_____
_____
_____
_____
_____

⚓ Truth Basic Training Verses

Carefully study the following verses by reading the scripture in various translations, including the King James Version; underline any words that stand out to you; use a Strong's Concordance, which is an index of every word in the King James Version, and read the entire chapter of the verse. Journal your notes and summary.

"Stand fast therefore in the liberty wherewith Christ has made us free and be not entangled again with the yoke of bondage." Galatians 5:1

_____

_____

_____

_____

_____

_____

_____

"No man can serve two masters: for either he will hate the one and love the other; or else he will hold to the one and despise the other. You cannot serve God and mammon." Matthew 6:24

_____

_____

_____

_____

_____

_____

_____

_____

CHAPTER 8

BRINGING HEAVEN TO EARTH (PRAYER)

I started writing down my dreams and began to recognize how God was speaking to me in my dreams. He was giving me revelation in my dreams for situations that were occurring in my life. He was leading me to intercede for others in prayer. In one dream, God revealed to me a way to escape from a potentially harmful situation. He revealed to me a way of escape from the enemy's trap.

I was involved in a group for a specific goal and purpose. I started hearing statements in this group that concerned me. At this point, there had been about three different situations that caused me concern because of incorrect statements and views within this group. I had a very specific dream about this group, the bad seeds (false statements) that were being planted (spoken) in the group, and the danger of being around these falsehoods. Through my dream, the LORD relayed to me the dangers if I remained associating myself with this group. The dream was giving me a way of escape from evil and prayer strategies. I followed through with the LORD's guidance to remove myself from this group, and I am very grateful for His guidance and protection. When we are abiding in a close relationship with the LORD, our discernment will be sharp. We will recognize evil and lies, and thereby, we will be praying the will of God.

As you delve into this chapter on **Your Journey to Truth** of prayer, you will reflect on your prayer strategy, the different types of prayers, knowing your spiritual authority and how to use it in prayer, and how your prayers can be hindered.

👣 YOUR JOURNEY TO TRUTH

<u>THE PRAYER IN FAITH MOVES MOUNTAINS</u>

1. After reading Chapter 8 of *Called to Truth, A Practical, Biblical Guide to Spiritual & Physical Wholeness*, journal your description of prayer. In your description, include the importance of praying in faith.

_____

_____

_____

_____

_____

_____

_____

_____

_____

_____

2. <u>Listed below are the different types of prayers discussed in Chapter 8.</u> Next to the prayer, journal your thoughts as to when this prayer is best used and how you would describe that prayer model:

Prayer of faith:

_____

_____

_____

_____

_____

_____

_____

Prayer of agreement:

_____

_____

_____

_____

_____

_____

Binding and loosing prayer (to bind is to fasten, prohibit, forbid) (to loose is to unbind, set free from):

Intercessory prayer:

Praising and thanking God in prayer:

Praying in tongues:

The LORD's Prayer:

_____
_____
_____
_____
_____
_____
_____
_____

Prayers from the heart:

_____
_____
_____
_____
_____
_____
_____
_____

Spiritual warfare prayer:

_____
_____
_____
_____
_____
_____
_____

3. The Word of God and Prayer

a.) Do you think your prayer will be answered if you are praying for things that you do not have understanding for or revelation of in the word of God?

_____
_____

b.) Can you have faith for things that you don't understand in the word of God?

_____
_____
_____

_____
_____
_____
_____
_____

4. Let's review GOD'S ORDER IN PRAYER on page 37 _of Called to Truth,_
A Practical, Biblical Guide to Spiritual & Physical Wholeness.

a.) What is the believer's spiritual authority?

_____
_____
_____
_____
_____
_____
_____
_____

b.) What are the ways your prayers can be hindered?

_____
_____
_____
_____
_____
_____
_____
_____
_____
_____
_____

c.) Are you waiting on God or is God waiting on you? Is your prayer in faith
(without doubt and unbelief)? Journal your thoughts.

_____
_____
_____
_____

_____
_____
_____
_____

d.) What should you do if you have doubt and unbelief when praying? For further explanation, read Hebrews 11:6 and Romans 10:17.

_____
_____
_____
_____
_____
_____
_____
_____
_____
_____
_____

5. Now we will look at page 37-39, <u>THE WORD OF GOD IS SHARPER THAN ANY TWO-EDGED SWORD.</u>

a.) Praying using the Word of God is extremely powerful. On the lines below, write out the Bible verse Hebrews 4:12. In your own words, summarize these powerful words.

_____
_____
_____
_____
_____
_____
_____
_____

b.) Through your spiritual authority as a believer in Jesus Christ, write a decree for your life. See the description of a decree and the two examples from page 38 of _Called to Truth, A Practical, Biblical Guide to Spiritual & Physical Wholeness._

_____
_____
_____

_____
_____
_____
_____
_____
_____
_____

c.) Write out your own spiritual warfare prayer referencing the examples on page 38.

_____
_____
_____
_____
_____
_____
_____
_____
_____

d.) If you pray before meals regularly, this question is probably not necessary, but it is surprising how many forget to do this. I highly recommend a new commitment to what God has indicated in His word; pray for Him to bless your food before you eat. Journal your response to the following question: Why is praying before meals important? See pages 39-40 and the verses included in the section, "Pray over your food."

_____
_____
_____
_____
_____
_____
_____
_____

6. A disciple is a follower of Jesus Christ and one who studies the word of God for their life. Why are disciples to fast and pray according to page 40-41 of "FASTING AND PRAYER?"

_____

_____
_____
_____
_____
_____
_____
_____

7. After reading PERSONAL TESTIMONY–THE POWER OF PRAYER from pages 41-42, record some of your answered prayers. Reflect on your answered prayers! Your testimony of God's goodness and faithfulness will strengthen you and purify your faith (remove doubt and unbelief).

_____
_____
_____
_____
_____
_____
_____
_____
_____

8. Listed above, we reviewed the different types of prayers. Journal below a prayer list. Include the type of prayer model you will use and who you will be praying for.

_____
_____
_____
_____
_____
_____
_____
_____
_____
_____

_____

_____

⚓ Truth Basic Training Verses

Carefully study the following verses by reading the scripture in various translations, including the King James Version; underline any words that stand out to you; use a Strong's Concordance which is an index of every word in the King James Version, and read the entire chapter of the verse. Journal your notes and summary.

"And when they had prayed, the place was shaken where they were assembled together; and they were all filled with the Holy Ghost, and they spoke the word of God with boldness." *Acts 4:31*

_____
_____
_____
_____
_____
_____
_____
_____
_____

CHAPTER 9

•————— ❧ —————•

OUR SUPERPOWER; THE POWER OF FAITH

Doubt and unbelief had saturated my soul. To wipe out doubt and unbelief, I needed to flood my soul and spirit with the word of God and teachings on faith. I listened to many teachings on faith to allow the truth from the word of God to penetrate my inner being (my mind, soul, and spirit). When you search the word of God with your whole heart, you will saturate yourself with truth and it will speak life to you and lead you to exercise your faith. Your faith is like a muscle; when you use it, it is strengthened. While going through difficult trials in my life, I needed to take up or raise up my faith because it was my shield that extinguishes all the fiery darts of the wicked. These trials are opportunities for our faith to be purified. When our faith goes through the fire, it is purified. I can attest that my faith is purer having gone through trials.

Our faith can only go as far as we have had revelation. For example, if you are praying for something from scripture you don't understand or have no revelation of, it is going to be very difficult to receive what you don't understand or believe. For example, if someone says they believe in Jesus, but they don't believe He is the Son of God, then how could they receive the promise from John 3:16. *"For God so loved the world, that He gave His only begotten Son, that whosoever believeth in Him should not perish, but have everlasting life."* Therefore, when you combine your faith (without doubt and unbelief) with the revelatory truth of the word of God, your prayers will move mountains!

An example of this in my life was when I was baptized. At my baptism, I knew I needed to renounce and rebuke fear in my life. Right before I was baptized, I gave a testimony of how I was rebuking fear in my life. I declared, understood, and had revelation of Second Timothy 1:7, *"For God hath not given us the spirit of fear; but of power, and of love, and of a sound mind.*" I applied my faith to this verse and that day there was a wrestling match for my deliverance. They had to immerse me again because they couldn't completely immerse me the first time. God's truth prevailed as I applied my faith to defeating fear in my life. The spirit of fear had to leave as my faith spoke that day and fear was drowned out. We have authority over evil in our lives as we walk in truth! Come along on **Your Journey to Truth** to use your authority over evil in your life and walk by faith.

YOUR JOURNEY TO TRUTH

FAITH IS YOUR SHIELD. ABOVE ALL, TAKING THE SHIELD OF FAITH

As followers of Jesus Christ, we are to fight the good fight of faith, which is to contend with the enemy of sin, lies, Satan, fear, doubt, and unbelief. With faith, there will be an action which will reveal your faith. The same applies if you are fearful; your actions will reveal fear.

There was a time when our family needed to move to another state, but no doors had opened for this to happen yet. Therefore, I agree with the word of God and what Philippians 4:19 said, *"But my God shall supply all your need according to His riches in glory by Christ Jesus."* His word says He supplies all our needs, and this was a need for our family. Therefore, I agreed with the word of God and began activating my faith before there was any physical evidence of our family moving. I prepared my home to get ready to sell. Our swimming pool needed a major repair, and I scheduled the repair. I began going through our belongings and taking things to Goodwill™. I began packing items in boxes. Within about a year, my husband had a job relocation to another state! I have seen the LORD's goodness repeatedly as I trust Him.

There are other faith battles in which I continue to fight and take up my shield of faith. There is no expiration date on our faith; I will keep standing. Let's continue to fight the good fight of faith, finish our assignment, and keep the faith!

After reading Chapter 9 of *Called to Truth, A Practical, Biblical Guide to Spiritual & Physical Wholeness*, answer the questions below.

FAITH QUESTIONS:

1. Who do you trust for your daily provisions?

_____

_____

2. Do the choices you make reveal you have faith in God?

_____
_____
_____
_____

3. Are you embarrassed or timid in your faith of the Lord Jesus Christ?

_____
_____
_____
_____
_____

4.What evidence is there in your life that you trust God with your life?

_____
_____
_____
_____
_____
_____
_____
_____
_____

FAITH VERSUS FEAR

Journal any evidence of fear in your life.

_____
_____
_____
_____
_____
_____
_____
_____
_____
_____

RENEW YOUR MIND: If you have meditated long enough on fear, you have made a pathway for fear. You need to recognize how fear has gained access in your mind and rebuke it. You renew your mind with the word of God. Follow the steps below to rebuke fear in your life and renew your mind:

STEP 1: Recognize that fear is a liar. Recognize how fear entered your life. As you examine your life, journal the entry points of fear. Examine your thoughts, attitudes, and your choices and if they were influenced by fear.

_____
_____
_____
_____
_____
_____
_____
_____
_____
_____
_____
_____
_____
_____
_____
_____
_____

STEP 2: Speak to your fear: "Fear I rebuke and renounce you, you have no place here, get out fear!" Journal your declaration to rebuke and renounce fear in your life.

_____
_____
_____
_____
_____
_____
_____
_____

_____
_____
_____
_____
_____
_____
_____

STEP 3: Repentance is a change of mind. Journal how you have changed your mind and have recognized fear as a liar and that you choose to walk by faith.

_____
_____
_____
_____
_____
_____
_____
_____
_____
_____

STEP 4: Recognizing stumbling blocks: Make a list of the areas in your life in which you will guard your heart and mind from agreeing with fear.

_____
_____
_____
_____
_____
_____
_____
_____
_____
_____

STEP 5: Search the Bible for scripture verses that rebuke and renounce the fear you are removing from your life. Below are some examples of scripture verses you can use as declarations of faith: 2 Timothy 1:7; Psalm 18:2; Hebrews 11:6; Romans 10:17; Hebrews 11:1; Mark 11:22-24; Ephesians 2:8-9; Proverbs 3:5-6; Luke 1:37; Philippians 4:13; John 3:16, and many more.

After searching the scriptures, record the scriptures you will use as prayers of faith declarations.

_____
_____
_____
_____
_____
_____
_____
_____
_____
_____
_____
_____

STEP 6: Speak the above truths you found in scripture and continue to meditate on them until they become planted in your mind and heart. Continue to recognize, renounce, and repent for any fear that tries to reenter your life. Journal your notes.

_____
_____
_____
_____
_____
_____
_____
_____
_____
_____
_____
_____
_____
_____
_____
_____
_____
_____

PRAYING IN FAITH

The last section of Chapter 9 is "PRAYING IN FAITH." Our faith is vitally important to every aspect of the believer's walk, including prayer. Our faith can be infected with doubt and unbelief by receiving negative thoughts, by hearing and receiving negative reports, by believing lies, by agreeing with fear, etc. We need to be careful what we let into our mind and soul.

1. Journal scripture verses and Bible stories giving the evidence of someone who walked by faith. In Hebrews 11 you will find many examples of believer's who walked by faith.

_____
_____
_____
_____
_____
_____
_____
_____
_____
_____
_____

2. Journal a testimony of an answered prayer.

_____
_____
_____
_____
_____
_____
_____
_____
_____
_____
_____
_____

3. Through trials our faith is tested and purified by fire. Journal a time when you have gone through a trial and how your faith was tested.

_____
_____
_____
_____
_____
_____
_____
_____

⚓ Truth Basic Training Verses

Carefully study the following verses by reading the scripture in various translations, including the King James Version; underline any words that stand out to you; use a Strong's Concordance, which is an index of every word in the King James Version, and read the entire chapter of the verse. Journal your notes and summary.

"Above all, taking the shield of faith, wherewith you shall be able to quench all the fiery darts of the wicked." Ephesians 6:16

_____
_____
_____
_____
_____
_____
_____

"Jesus said to him, 'If you can believe, all things are possible to him that believes.'" Mark 9:23

_____
_____
_____
_____
_____
_____

CHAPTER 10

OUR GUIDE

I really had little understanding of the Holy Spirit until I was in my thirties. The Holy Spirit led me into truth by urging me to walk in obedience. I remember the process of the Holy Spirit urging me to confront evil in my life. My faith was purified when I walked in obedience. I saw how the Holy Spirit led me when I walked <u>through</u> the valley of the shadow of death, and I was not to fear. Evil can seem like a consuming fire until you defeat it and find that with God all things are possible.

My journey with the Holy Spirit became increasingly more powerful as I was water baptized and then years later I was prayed over and received the baptism of the Holy Spirit. I am exceedingly grateful that the Holy Spirit has given me deeper understanding of the word of God. The Holy Spirit has given me the strength to do things I could have never done in my own strength. The Holy Spirit has given me the joy of the LORD. The joy I have is quite different from the world's happiness. I want to learn more about Jesus all the time, and I am blessed to experience His joyous adventure when I follow Him! The Holy Spirit has been my lifeguard and my life guide: He has kept me from drowning in life's circumstances and He has placed me on the mountain top.

The Holy Spirit led me out of being deceived, led me out of being manipulated by witchcraft, and led me out of being held captive by fear. Others may not know what evil someone is going through on the inside, but the Holy Spirit knows and is ready to lead us to freedom. Come along on **Your Journey to Truth**.

👣 YOUR JOURNEY TO TRUTH

<u>DO YOU KNOW THE SPIRIT OF TRUTH? (The Holy Spirit)</u>

1. After reading Chapter 10 of *Called to Truth, A Practical, Biblical Guide to Spiritual & Physical Wholeness*, who is the Holy Spirit?

_____

_____

_____

_____

_____

_____

_____

_____

_____

_____

2. Journal what knowledge you have gained about the Holy Spirit. Write below any questions for which you are seeking God for further understanding about the Holy Spirit.

_____

_____

_____

_____

_____

_____

_____

_____

_____

_____

_____

_____

3. <u>Journal your testimony of the Holy Spirit in your life.</u>

a.) Journal a testimony of the Holy Spirit guiding you in your life.

_____

_____

_____
_____
_____
_____
_____
_____

b.) Journal a testimony of the Holy Spirit leading you into truth and giving you the strength to be obedient.

_____
_____
_____
_____
_____
_____
_____

c.) Journal your testimony of the Holy Spirit teaching you discernment (understanding, recognize truth and lies).

_____
_____
_____
_____
_____
_____
_____

d.) Journal your testimony of the Holy Spirit's healing and deliverance power in your life.

_____
_____
_____
_____
_____
_____
_____
_____

e.) Journal your water baptism testimony.

_____
_____

_____
_____
_____
_____
_____
_____
_____

f.) Journal below the gifts of the Holy Spirit discussed on page 50 of *Called to Truth, A Practical, Biblical Guide to Spiritual & Physical Wholeness*. What is the purpose of these gifts?

_____
_____
_____
_____
_____
_____
_____
_____
_____
_____
_____
_____

g.) After reading about the baptism of the Holy Spirit on pages 48-50 of *Called to Truth, A Practical, Biblical Guide to Spiritual & Physical Wholeness*, journal your understanding of the baptism of the Holy Spirit. What is the purpose of the baptism of the Holy Spirit? Journal your testimony of the baptism of the Holy Spirit or any questions for which you are seeking God for understanding about the baptism of the Holy Spirit.

_____
_____
_____
_____
_____
_____
_____
_____

_____

_____

4. Through the power of the Holy Spirit, there is power to change your life and others. We are not to deny the power of the Holy Spirit that works through believers. After reading page 51-52 of _Called to Truth, A Practical, Biblical Guide to Spiritual & Physical Wholeness_, journal your thoughts and answers on the following questions:

a.) If you deny the power of the Holy Spirit, how is this a stumbling block?

_____

_____

_____

_____

_____

_____

_____

b.) What can cause a hindrance to us hearing the Holy Spirit?

_____

_____

_____

_____

_____

_____

c.) Do you hear the Holy Spirit guiding you, comforting you, and bringing you truth? If not, what do you think may be causing the hindrance to you hearing the Holy Spirit?

_____

_____

_____

_____

_____

_____

_____

5. How has the Holy Spirit empowered you in your life? Journal the times in your life when you had breakthrough and victory because you followed the Holy Spirit (pages 52-53 of _Called to Truth, A Practical, Biblical Guide to Spiritual & Physical Wholeness_).

_____
_____
_____
_____
_____
_____
_____
_____
_____
_____
_____
_____
_____
_____
_____
_____

6. After reading the six tests to help you recognize God's voice and the leading of the Holy Spirit on page 53 of *Called to Truth, A Practical, Biblical Guide to Spiritual & Physical Wholeness*, journal your summary of recognizing God's voice.

_____
_____
_____
_____
_____
_____
_____
_____
_____
_____
_____
_____
_____
_____
_____
_____
_____
_____

⚓ Truth Basic Training Verses

Carefully study the following verses by reading the scripture in various translations, including the King James Version; underline any words that stand out to you; use a Strong's Concordance, which is an index of every word in the King James Version, and read the entire chapter of the verse. Journal your notes and summary.

"Even the Spirit of truth; whom the world cannot receive, because it sees Him not, neither knows Him: but you know Him; for He dwells with you, and shall be in you." John 14:17

_____

_____

_____

_____

_____

_____

_____

_____

_____

_____

_____

"For if you live after the flesh, you shall die: but if you through the Spirit do mortify the deeds of the body, you shall live." Romans 8:13

_____

_____

_____

_____

_____

_____

_____

_____

CHAPTER 11

---◆❀◆---

SATAN AND HIS EVIL KINGDOM

ARE YOU UNAWARE OF SATAN'S DEVICES?

The only Bible truths I remember hearing about Satan in my earlier years, was when he tempted Eve in the Garden and when he tempted Jesus in the desert. I had never thought much about Satan and his schemes and devices against me. In my small understanding of the spiritual world, I guess I assumed Satan was too busy attacking the important people, which he probably is, but he had an entire evil kingdom at his disposal.

Regardless of my ignorance of the plans and devices of Satan and his evil kingdom, I was still his prey. I had little understanding of the evil spiritual realm. When the darkness was surrounding me, I asked God to show me the truth. I went to the LORD completely open to whatever He needed to teach me.

This is one vision I had years ago and again more recently: I saw a secret passageway within the walls of a house. Out of the secret passageways, from behind the walls, evil spirits were moving about and searching for human beings to torment and embody. They kept themselves hidden in the corridors and many were not aware of their existence or how they got access to these passageways. They want to stay hidden; they do not want to be exposed. Come along on **Your Journey to Truth** to expose the evil operating in your life and remove it.

👣 YOUR JOURNEY TO TRUTH

OUR ENEMY: THE KINGDOM OF DARKNESS

After reading Chapter 11 of *Called to Truth, A Practical, Biblical Guide to Spiritual & Physical Wholeness*, what experiences have you had in which you can now recognize that the kingdom of darkness was at work, and your battle was not with a person?

_____

_____

_____

_____

_____

_____

_____

_____

_____

_____

_____

_____

TACTICS OF SATAN AND HIS EVIL KINGDOM

1. Bondage is being a slave to sin, lies, and evil. Freedom is being free from slavery and thereby having liberty. Those who have been made free can tell you what it was like to be a slave and what it is now like to be free. By applying our faith to the completed work of Jesus Christ, we overcome evil.

To help you further determine whether you are walking in bondage, I will explain a little of my story. In my years of bondage, I did not love myself and did not even know I was supposed to love myself. I lived my life in fear. I was walking around with some type of heaviness on me, and somehow my free will had been hijacked because I believed I had no choices. Receiving my freedom in Christ meant I had found the truth and had revelation of it. Receiving my freedom in Christ meant I was now living my life to please God and not man. I was no longer a slave to Satan's lies because I was no longer ignorant of Satan's devices. I came to the knowledge of the truth that I had to fight and resist Satan because he would try to steal the plans God has for me. Journal the evidence in your life of freedom or bondage.

_____
_____
_____
_____
_____
_____
_____
_____
_____

2. Examine any area of your life where fear has entered. Journal the type of fear (example: fear of the future, fear of death, fear of loneliness, etc.) or any area of your life in which fear has entered. Determine the entry point of fear. Examine how your life changed after fear entered. The longer fear has been around, the harder it can be to detect because it has become a part of your life. Pray for revelation and to rebuke and renounce the fear that gained access in your life.

_____
_____
_____
_____
_____
_____
_____
_____
_____

3. Have you been sober (clear judgment) and vigilant (alert, watchful to avoid danger) not allowing Satan access to you or your life?

a.) Temptations and evil can enter through your senses. Are you protecting your senses: what you see, what you hear, what you smell, what you touch or what touches you, or what you taste? List which of your senses you have not been protecting but need to guard. List how you will guard your senses.

_____
_____
_____
_____

_____
_____
_____
_____
_____
_____
_____
_____

b.) Are you protecting your body, your mind, and your heart from evil and temptation? Examine which of these areas you need to guard more vigilantly. Satan knows our weak areas, and we need to make wise choices in those areas. <u>Journal your plan to guard and protect your body, your mind, and your heart from falling into temptation.</u>

_____
_____
_____
_____
_____
_____
_____
_____
_____
_____

WARNING: SIN AND THE OPEN DOOR

1. Below is a checklist to help locate and expose the areas that Satan has easy access in your life as explained on page 59 of *Called to Truth, A Practical, Biblical Guide to Spiritual & Physical Wholeness*. If you make a checkmark on a question with a list, underline the specific item that is a problem area. I suggest reading each scripture listed below. The word of God is alive and active, and it will expose lies and reveal truth in your life.

_____Am I following the world's way? (Ephesian 2:2)

_____Am I seeking ungodly counsel. For example, astrologers, palm readers, trusting in men to tell me my future, superstitions? (Isaiah 47:13-14, 1 Samuel 28:1-25, Acts 16:16-19)

_____Am I engaging in any divination, witchcraft, sorcery, consulter of the dead, or fortune teller (familiar spirits meaning a wizard, a conjurer)?

(Deut.18:9-14, 1 Chronicles 10:13-14, I Samuel 28:1-25, Isaiah 8:19, Acts 16:16-19, Leviticus 20:6)

_____Am I fearful, unbelieving, abominable, murderer, whoremonger, sorcerer, idolater, or liar? (Revelation 21:8)

_____Have I put other gods before the one true God? Am I worshipping or serving any idols or other gods? Am I using God's name in a perverse way? Am I not remembering God's holy day? Have I dishonored my father and mother, have I killed, have I committed adultery, have I stolen, have I spoken lies against my neighbor, or have I coveted anything that is my neighbors? (Exodus 20:1-17)

_____Am I being unwise and listening to a sorcerer which is a false prophet? (Acts 13:6-8)

_____Am I departing from the faith, giving heed to seducing spirits and doctrines of devils, speaking lies in hypocrisy, having my conscience seared with a hot iron, forbidding to marry, and commanding to abstain from certain kinds of food which God has created to be received with thanksgiving of them who believe and know the truth? (1 Timothy 4:1-3)

_____I do not love God with **all** my heart, I do not love God will **all** my soul, and I do not love God with **all** my mind. I do not love myself and do not love my neighbor as myself? (Matthew 22:37-40)

_____Am I practicing sinning and willingly continuing in sin without repenting? (Isaiah 59:2)

_____Am I wise in my own eyes and do not fear God? (Proverbs 3:7)

_____Am I not sober (clear judgment) and not vigilant in my life? (I Peter 5:8)

_____Have I not forgiven myself or someone else? (Matthew 6:14-15, Matthew 18:21-35)

_____Do I have problems with anger? (Ephesians 4:26-27)

_____Are any of the following activities part of my lifestyle: yoga, Reiki healers, New Age, acupuncture, hypnotism, manipulation, and domination, and many more? See pages 59-61 of *Called to Truth, a Practical, Biblical Guide to Spiritual & Physical Wholeness* for more detail and more scriptures that are not listed here.

This list is a tool to examine yourself; it is not all inclusive and is not about condemnation. It is about looking in the mirror and asking God to cleanse us of all unrighteousness. *"Search me, O God, and know my heart: try me, and know my thoughts: and see if there be any wicked way in me, and lead me in the way everlasting."* (Psalm 139:23-24)

2. After reading page 59, below are steps to help guide a wounded soul to healing and restoration (an ache/hurt in your heart that won't go away, damage done to your emotions which affect your decisions):

a.) Write a letter to the LORD explaining your true feelings about the hurt that led to your wounded soul.

_____

_____

_____

_____

_____

_____

_____

_____

_____

_____

_____

b.) Jesus has borne our griefs and carried our sorrows. Borne is to take away, carried off, and swept away. Griefs are calamity and disease. Carried is to bear and take the load. Sorrows are any type of pain, anguish, affliction, and grief. Jesus has borne your grief and carried your sorrow. Release your pain to Him by releasing your pain out of your belly and receive in His healing love. (Isaiah 53:4-5)

c.) Release any bitterness or unforgiveness out of your belly. If there is something you have shame or guilt about, release it out of your belly and be free by receiving the freedom Jesus bought and paid for.

d.) Pray and receive the LORD's healing touch through the completed work of Jesus on the cross. Through Jesus's stripes you are healed. (Isaiah 53:5, Psalm 147:3, Psalm 107:20)

e.) Search the word of God for verses that speak life to your soul and declare them out loud. Journal the scripture verses you will pray and declare.

_____

_____

_____

_____

_____

_____
_____
_____
_____
_____
_____
_____
_____
_____
_____
_____
_____
_____
_____

3. Let's now look at page 60 of *Called to Truth, A Practical, Biblical Guide to Spiritual & Physical Wholeness* regarding handling strife or conflict in the home. Strife is a disagreement that arises, increases with intensity, and can lead to a bitter disagreement with high emotions of anger. When there is a pattern of strife, there can be repetitive triggers that cause disagreements that can lead to soul hurts. Therefore, a plan of action should be put into place to work through the root cause of the strife. Pray for wisdom and devise a plan to work through the root cause of the strife. Journal below your action plan which should include scripture verses to apply in prayer to the situation, and a step-by-step strategy plan of handling the situation with truth and love being guided by the Holy Spirit.

_____
_____
_____
_____
_____
_____
_____
_____
_____
_____
_____
_____

_____
_____

4. Speaking Idle (careless) Words

a.) After reading page 60 of *Called to Truth, A Practical, Biblical Guide to Spiritual & Physical Wholeness* on idle words, do you feel this is a problem for you?

_____
_____
_____
_____
_____

b.) Do you speak careless words about yourself and others?

_____
_____
_____
_____
_____
_____

c. Let's develop a strategy plan to prevent idle words. Journal the careless words you commonly speak, ask family members what careless words you speak, determine what type of situations cause you to speak careless words, and begin replacing those careless words with "words of life".

_____
_____
_____
_____
_____
_____
_____
_____
_____

JESUS OUR AUTHORITY

After reading pages 61-63 of *Called to Truth, A Practical, Biblical Guide to Spiritual & Physical Wholeness*, you will journal how to use your authority as a believer in Jesus Christ to take intentional steps to walk in truth. You disarm Satan's plans for your life by following God's ways and His order. Develop your personal plan by using your authority as a believer to kick lies, sin, and Satan out of your life. You have the choice to be intentional every day in the decisions you make. The following is a list of ideas you may want to include in your strategy plan. You may want to write out certain scripture verses to decree over your life; you may want to start a Bible study in your home; you may want to plan a time daily to talk to God about whatever is on your mind; you may want to intentionally write out steps to get your life back on track; you may want to call that person toward whom you had bitterness and tell them you are sorry; you may want to start a family time where you share God testimonies with each other, or maybe it will simply be one step you can make to get closer to God. Journal your strategy plan to live an intentional life of truth seeking.

_____

_____

_____

_____

_____

_____

_____

_____

_____

_____

_____

_____

_____

_____

_____

_____

_____

_____

_____

_____

_____

_____

_____

_____

_____

_____

_____

PERSONAL TESTMONY

1. Before moving onto Chapter 12, it is important we review my testimony from page 63 of *Called to Truth, A Practical, Biblical Guide to Spiritual & Physical Wholeness*. In reference to my testimony of my past participation with yoga, we will look at counterfeit powers. The Holy Spirit is the Spirit of Truth and is the power in the believer's life to walk in truth. But there is a counterfeit power from Satan that believers need to be aware of. As we look at this, we must be careful, because we are not to deny the power of the Holy Spirit, but we need to be aware that Satan will try to bring counterfeit powers into our life.

In Second Corinthians 11: 4 (amplified), *"For [you seem willing to allow it] if one comes and preaches another Jesus whom we have not preached, or if you receive a different spirit from the one you accepted. You tolerate all this beautifully [welcoming the deception]."* God has given believer's the spirit of power from Second Timothy 1:7 which is the Holy Spirit. You can also review Second Corinthians 11:13-14 describing how Satan transformed into an angel of light, and that there are false and deceitful workers disguised at workers for Christ. Stay vigilant because we are to discern good and evil.

A friend of mine had an unbeliever come into her home and pray for her about pain she was having. She told me her pain went away instantly. Satan loves to use his power to deceive and will bring some relief to us. When I did yoga, I had some relief from anxiety, but it was only temporary, and it was from the father of lies and not the Spirit of Truth. The Holy Spirit is my Healer and has healed the damage that yoga did in my life.

Journal your testimony of the power of the Holy Spirit and how to be vigilant in recognizing the father of lies (Satan) and his schemes.

_____

_____

_____

_____

_____

_____
_____
_____
_____
_____
_____
_____
_____
_____
_____
_____
_____

⚓ Truth Basic Training Verses

Carefully study the following verses by reading the scripture in various translations, including the King James Version; underline any words that stand out to you; use a Strong's Concordance which is an index of every word in the King James Version, and read the entire chapter of the verse. Journal your notes and summary.

"Lest Satan should get an advantage of us: for we are not ignorant of his devices." 2 Corinthians 2:11

_____
_____
_____
_____
_____
_____

"Now the serpent was more subtle than any beast of the field which the LORD God had made. And he said to the woman, 'Has God indeed said, You shall not eat of every tree of the garden'?" Genesis 3:1

_____
_____
_____
_____

CHAPTER 12

DON'T BE DECEIVED

Seeking scripture will reveal truths that give us wisdom and discernment to detect lies and deliver us out of the hands of Satan. Second Timothy 4:4 warns about those who turn from the truth to listen to stories, myths, and fables. As you seek His truths and follow them, you will be delivered out of the hands of Satan's lying stories, and out of his deceptive myths and fables.

The world will try to puff us up, try to tell us we are somebody we are not, and the world will try to steal our time, our treasure, and our talent. Our time is precious, our choices are precious, and our discernment is priceless. We need to exercise our discernment to strengthen this gift. If we become passive, evil can gain a foothold.

"Woe to them that call evil good, and good evil; that put darkness for light, and light for darkness; that put bitter for sweet, and sweet for bitter!" (Isaiah 5:20) As the values of the world have deteriorated, we can't deteriorate in our beliefs. If the followers of Jesus Christ don't recognize what is good and what is evil, who will? I had an encounter with someone recently who didn't want to call Satan evil because they felt we were supposed to be kind to Satan.

Recognizing what is good and what is evil is not according to each person's opinion, it is according to God and His word. Therefore, having the knowledge of the word of God in our minds and hearts is essential in discerning good and evil. God created us with a conscience to know right from wrong but if we slip into doing things against our conscience, our conscience will not be sharp, and we will be deceived. It is like a knife that hasn't been sharpened in a long time, it isn't sharp enough to cut through the lies and deceptions of the world anymore.

Don't be deceived! We are not to be spectators of the evil going on in our own life. We are each responsible for our life and what is happening in it. There is a stand you will need to make in your life against evil. Draw a line in the sand and make a commitment to war against your wrong thinking and your bad actions. Satan wants you to think you have no power to overcome, but that is a lie from the pits of hell. You are a warrior who will overcome, but you must take a stand in your life and not be passive. Come along on **Your Journey to Truth** of overcoming evil in your life.

YOUR JOURNEY TO TRUTH

DISCERN GOOD AND EVIL

Within Chapter 12 of *Called to Truth, A Practical, Biblical Guide to Spiritual & Physical Wholeness*, there are fourteen different "DON'T BE DECEIVED" sections. For each section, journal the truth revealed within that section.

1. _____
   _____
   _____
   _____
   _____
   _____
   _____

2. _____
   _____
   _____
   _____
   _____
   _____
   _____

3. _____
   _____
   _____
   _____
   _____
   _____
   _____

4. _____
   _____
   _____

5. _____

6. _____

7. _____

8. _____

9. _____

10. _____
_____
_____
_____
_____
_____
_____

11. _____
_____
_____
_____
_____
_____
_____
_____

12. _____
_____
_____
_____
_____
_____
_____
_____

13. _____
_____
_____
_____
_____
_____
_____
_____

14. _____
_____
_____
_____
_____
_____
_____

Journal your strategy plan to continue seeking God's truth and exercising your discernment.

_____
_____

_____
_____
_____
_____
_____
_____
_____
_____

⚓ Truth Basic Training Verses

Carefully study the following verses by reading the scripture in various translations, including the King James Version; underline any words that stand out to you; use a Strong's Concordance which is an index of every word in the King James Version, and read the entire chapter of the verse. Journal your notes and summary.

"But strong meat belongs to them that are of full age, even those who by reason of use have their senses exercised to discern both good and evil." Hebrews 5:14

_____
_____
_____
_____
_____
_____
_____

CHAPTER 13

SPIRITUAL ROOTS

Uncover your Spiritual Roots to discover truth. What Spiritual Roots are hidden in your family tree? A father or mother can leave an inheritance of money to their children or an inheritance of debt. Unforeseen to some, a father or mother can leave their children a spiritual inheritance of blessings or curses. If you have never studied or understood generational iniquity, blessings, and curses, I recommend reading and studying these scriptures: Exodus 34:7, Numbers 14:18, Exodus 20:5-6, Deuteronomy 11:26-28, Deuteronomy 28, Deuteronomy 30, Deuteronomy 24:16, and Galatians 3:13.

I attended a ministry conference a few years ago and want to share with you this story as an example of manifesting bad fruit from generational Spiritual Roots. A mother and her adult child were in attendance at the conference. The mother's adult child manifested an extreme anger outburst that I would define as rage. The mother wanted to help her daughter and her daughter also wanted help, but when this outburst happened it was uncontrollable. The mother later indicated that she had often spoken word curses over her daughter. There were repetitive family patterns of word curses and bad decision-making over the years. Through years of spoken generational word curses, the family manifested much bad fruit. How does a family stop this cycle? We will delve deeper into this below. In summary: You recognize the truth about the situation; you renounce the agreement made with evil/the lie; you repent (change your mind and then change your behavior); you make an agreement with God's truth; you seek scripture to stand on in truth; you pray, and you use your authority to remove evil out of your family tree. Come along on **Your Journey to Truth** to uncover your Spiritual Roots to discover truth and renounce evil.

👣 YOUR JOURNEY TO TRUTH

1. After reading Chapter 13 of *Called to Truth, A Practical, Biblical Guide to Spiritual & Physical Wholeness*, journal a summary of the importance of forgiving others and ourselves. If you have anger towards God, towards yourself, or towards another person, now is the time to examine your heart and work through this with God. Journal scripture verses on forgiveness, how you are to love, and how God first loved you (1 John 4:18-21).

_____

_____

_____

_____

_____

_____

_____

_____

_____

2. As you meditate on Nehemiah 9, as discussed on page 70 of *Called to Truth, A Practical, Biblical Guide to Spiritual & Physical Wholeness*, journal a summary of these verses. From these verses, how can you remove your bad Spiritual Roots and secure your good Spiritual Roots?

_____

_____

_____

_____

_____

_____

_____

_____

_____

_____

3. **Spiritual Examination of the Family Tree** (refer to page 71 of *Called to Truth, A Practical, Biblical Guide to Spiritual & Physical Wholeness*): Beginning with **Step 1A,** you will **examine** your family tree.

First, through His completed work on the cross, Jesus has borne our griefs and carried our sorrows. He was wounded for our transgressions, was bruised for our iniquities, was punished for our peace, and with His stripes we are healed. Second, Jesus Christ has redeemed us from the curse of the law because He was made a curse for us. Third, the blessings of God are received by faith in Jesus's completed work on the cross. As we apply our faith to the word of God, we receive the blessings that Jesus bought and paid for on the cross. (Isaiah 53:4-5, Galatians 3)

According to Deuteronomy 5:9, *"Thou shalt not bow down thyself unto them, nor serve them: for I the LORD thy God am a jealous God, visiting the iniquity of the fathers upon the children unto the third and fourth generation of them that hate me."* In addition, Numbers 14:18 states, *"The LORD is longsuffering, and of great mercy, forgiving iniquity and transgression, and by no means clearing the guilty, visiting the iniquity of the fathers upon the children unto the third and fourth generation."*

We know that when we put our faith in Jesus Christ and believe Isaiah 53:4-5 that Jesus took away our griefs, carried our sorrows, was wounded for our transgressions, was bruised for our iniquities, was punished for our peace, and with His stripes we are healed. By your faith and repentance, you will pull out the evil Spiritual Roots that were planted through the generations of your family.

Complete the questions below after you have examined the fruit of your family tree. If you don't have the information you need to complete the questions, pray and ask God how He wants you to proceed with this process.

a. List any repeated patterns of mental health issues in your family tree.

_____

_____

_____

_____

_____

_____

_____

_____

b. List any repeated illnesses/sicknesses that have common traits in your family tree.

_____

_____

_____

_____

_____

_____

c. List any repeated patterns of criminal activity in your family tree.

_____

_____

_____

_____

_____

_____

d. List any repeated signs of lack or poverty in your family tree.

_____

_____

_____

_____

_____

_____

_____

e. List any repeated patterns of accidents, tragedies, early deaths, miscarriages, or barrenness in your family tree.

_____

_____

_____

_____

_____

_____

_____

f. List any repeated patterns of marriage break-ups or patterns of relationship problems in your family tree.

_____

_____

_____

_____

_____

_____

_____

g. List any repeated patterns of addictions in your family tree.

_____
_____
_____
_____
_____
_____

h. List any repeated iniquities that have followed your family tree, such as: unforgiveness, hatred, bitterness, etc.

_____
_____
_____
_____
_____
_____

i. Record below any additional unhealthy repeated patterns that are evident in your family tree that are not a blessing.

_____
_____
_____
_____
_____
_____
_____
_____

4. Therefore, if you have found bad fruit is being produced through your family tree, let's find out the cause. The Bible says there is not a curse without a cause.

You are entering the **Spiritual Diagnostic Room** which is **Step 1B**. This is where your discernment, the word of God, the Holy Spirit, and any information you have gathered about your family tree will be reviewed to find a diagnosis (Spiritual Root) to the problem. If you don't have the information you need to complete these steps, pray and ask God how He wants you to proceed with this process. These steps are only a guide to help you in your healing process.

Listed below are a few examples to help you understand the spiritual principles of how curses develop through the generational blood lines. As you seek God for the healing of your family tree, He will reveal truths to you. The family blood lines can have iniquity and curses that have been running their course for generations, therefore, be patient through the restoration process.

Example 1: If there has been a family history of rebellion, the word of God says it is as the sin of witchcraft. Witchcraft is divination. Witchcraft can be charms, spells, practice of magic, religious practice involving magic and affinity with nature, a pagan tradition, bewitching, or manipulating/controlling a person's free will. (1 Samuel 15:23)

Example 2: If there is a family history of stubbornness, the word of God says it is as an iniquity and idolatry. Idolatry is worshipping a false god. What has your generational line been worshipping other than the one true God? (1 Samuel 15:23)

Example 3: If there has been a family history of depression, an evil spirit of heaviness is the root cause. (Isaiah 61:3)

Example 4: If someone in your generational bloodline has made an agreement/covenant with Satan and his evil kingdom knowingly or in ignorance. One example of this is a secret organization or society where pledges are made. You cannot serve two masters. (Exodus 23:32-33, Exodus 34:12, Malachi 3:18)

Example 5: If there is a family history of serving other gods, this is a root cause of idolatry. Serving other gods is someone or something you put in high regard that has become what you worship. Who has your generational bloodlines served; what have they sowed into? (Exodus 20:3-6, Exodus 23:32-33)

Example 6: If there has been a family history of anxiety disorders, panic attacks, phobias, and others; this is most likely from a root cause of fear. (2 Timothy 1:7, 1 John 4:18)

Journal any information you have gathered that will be helpful in your spiritual healing process.

_____

_____

_____

_____

_____

_____

_____

_____

_____

_____

_____

Prayer, the word of God, and listening to the Holy Spirit will lead you in determining the Diagnosis of the Spiritual Root. Below is a list of possible Spiritual Root Diagnosis:

Spiritual Root of Iniquity	Spiritual Truth
Disobeying the LORD	Luke 6:43-49
Not fearing the LORD (love, honor, and obey; in awe of)	Proverbs 1:7, Proverbs 8:13
Not listening and obeying the voice of the LORD	Deuteronomy 28:1-2
Practicing sinning	1 John 3:9 (Amplified), Hebrews 10:26
Idolatry	Exodus 20:3-6, Colossians 3:5
Stubbornness is as iniquity and idolatry	1 Samuel 15:23
Abominations, divination, occult activities	Deuteronomy 18:10-12
Pride	Proverbs 16:18, Isaiah 66:2 (Amplified)
Unforgiveness towards self or others	Matthew 6:14-15
Unloving towards self or others	1 John 3:10
Dishonoring parents	Deuteronomy 27:16, Ephesians 6:1-3
Rebellion is as the sin of witchcraft	1 Samuel 15:23
Jealousy and envy	James 3:16, Proverbs 14:30
No sorrowful repentance	Revelation 2:5
Demonic infestation	Luke 10:19, Mark 16:17-18

| No relationship with Jesus | John 14:6, 1 John 3:8-9 |

(No personal testimony about Him)

Not remembering the LORD's day	Isaiah 58:13-14
Living under a word curse	Proverbs 18:21, Proverbs 26:2
Living in fear not faith	2 Timothy 1:7, Romans 10:17

After gathering family information from your generational bloodlines, identifying the common bad fruits produced, searching scripture verses, praying, and listening to the Holy Spirit. List the single or multiple diagnosis of the Spiritual Root of Iniquity Diagnosis:

_____
_____
_____
_____
_____
_____
_____
_____

5. The remaining steps are all part of the Spiritual Surgery to return the family tree back to its intended plan and purpose of producing good fruit. With Spiritual Surgery, be patient. As it took years for the bad fruit of the family tree to develop, it may take time for the transformation process of the renewing of the mind. Of course with God, the timing could be miraculous. Sometimes after a surgery, a person may have to return for a second surgery because the disease was not completely removed from the root. God is merciful and sometimes the process takes time because some lies have flowed through our blood lines for so long and need to be cleansed/washed clean. The renewing of the mind is usually not an overnight process.

You are moving onto **Step 2** of page 71 from *Called to Truth, A Practical, Biblical Guide to Spiritual & Physical Wholeness*, where you are going into **Spiritual Surgery** to remove the Spiritual Root causing the bad fruit. Now it is time to rebuke and renounce the Spiritual Root or Roots in your generational blood line, that is causing bad fruit to be produced, from Step 1B. To renounce is to reject and declare your abandonment from something. To rebuke is to make a correction or reproof. Therefore, journal your recognition of the Spiritual Root of Iniquity in your generational line and how it is against God's order and holiness.

_____
_____
_____
_____
_____
_____
_____
_____
_____
_____
_____

Now journal your declaration of renouncing the iniquity in your family blood line.

_____
_____
_____
_____
_____
_____
_____
_____
_____
_____
_____

6. We are now moving to **Step 3** which is repentance. **Repentance is a change of mind** which includes recognizing sin and sorrowfully repenting from the heart. If there are other family members who have been on this journey with you, their participation would be of great value. Earlier, I recommended reading Nehemiah 9 for an example of this step. Journal you and your family's "change of mind" statements. You and your family can write a prayer of repentance, or use Psalm 51 as a model, or let your hearts lead you into a prayer of repentance for the generational iniquity and curse.

_____
_____
_____
_____

_____
_____
_____
_____
_____
_____
_____
_____
_____
_____
_____
_____
_____
_____
_____
_____
_____
_____
_____
_____
_____

7. In **Step 4**, you will **use your spiritual authority** as a believer in Jesus Christ. You will name the iniquity (Spiritual Root) that was unveiled in your family line and come into agreement with the word of God that the curse is broken off according to Galatians 3:13, "*Christ hath redeemed us from the curse of the law, being made a curse for us: for it is written, cursed is every one that hangs on a tree.*" You can use the lines below to journal your declaration.

_____
_____
_____
_____
_____
_____
_____
_____
_____
_____
_____
_____
_____

_____
_____
_____
_____
_____
_____
_____
_____
_____
_____

8. In **Step 5**, you will **search scripture** for a verse that counters the iniquity (Spiritual Root) that traveled through your family tree. You are searching scripture for a verse of truth to counter the lie. For example, if your generational line has engaged in occult/divination activities, your truth statement could look something like this: According to First Samuel 15:23, rebellion is as the sin of witchcraft/divination. I rebuke and renounce rebelling against You LORD. I repent (a change of mind) for our participation in these evils. Your word says as obedient children according to First Peter 1:14-16 that I am not to walk in former ignorance and sin, but you have called me to be holy. Dear LORD lead me and my family into the healing and deliverance from generational iniquity and curses. You, dear LORD, are Holy and I honor You. Lead me into freedom and the way of everlasting. In Jesus name. Amen. Journal the scriptures you are believing for your generational freedom.

_____
_____
_____
_____
_____
_____
_____
_____
_____
_____

9. **Last**, the power of prayer, your agreement with the word of God in faith, and breaking any covenant made with the evil kingdom, brings heaven to earth. As you continue to study the word of God and have revelation, the renewing of your mind will remove incorrect thinking patterns that have

come through your blood line. As you continue praying, ask the LORD for the next step to move your family into the freedom and release from generational iniquities and curses. Journal the knowledge and wisdom God has given you for your generational freedom.

_____
_____
_____
_____
_____
_____
_____
_____
_____
_____
_____
_____
_____
_____
_____
_____

⚓ Truth Basic Training Verses

Carefully study the following verses by reading the scripture in various translations, including the King James Version; underline any words that stand out to you; use a Strong's Concordance, which is an index of every word in the King James Version, and read the entire chapter of the verse. Journal your notes and summary.

"Blessed is the man that trusts in the LORD, and whose hope the LORD is. For he shall be as a tree planted by the waters, and that spreads out her roots by the water, and shall not see when heat comes, but her leaf shall be green; and shall not be careful in the year of drought, neither shall cease from yielding fruit." Jeremiah 17:7-8

_____
_____
_____
_____
_____

CHAPTER 14

OUR SPIRITUAL AUTHORITY THROUGH JESUS CHRIST

Satan gains access to our lives when we sin and believe his lies. On the contrary, when you are following and obeying the Lord Jesus Christ, and believing and following His word, you have spiritual authority through Jesus Christ to do His kingdom work on earth.

I had a student in my classroom who regularly had rebellious behavior. After weeks of the same behavior from this student, I was led to take a different approach to the situation. I looked the student in the eyes and said, *"In the name of Jesus, stop."* Another child in the classroom spoke up and said to the rebellious child, *"Praise the LORD! Don't you know God is your Creator?"* The classroom atmosphere changed as we shut down the rebellion. When the child in the classroom came into agreement with me, together we used our authority to restore order in the classroom.

When I used my authority that day in the classroom, the other child spoke up and testified of God's goodness too. As a soldier (believer) of Jesus Christ, you have been deployed to use the authority given to you by Jesus Christ to bring heaven to earth. Come along on **Your Journey to Truth** to understand and use your spiritual authority through your faith in Jesus Christ.

YOUR JOURNEY TO TRUTH

After reading Chapter 14 of *Called to Truth, A Practical, Biblical Guide to Spiritual & Physical Wholeness*, let's dissect the truths for further understanding of your authority through Jesus Christ.

OUR SPIRITUAL AUTHORITY: VICTORIOUS THROUGH JESUS CHRIST

1. Testing your words: Death and life are in the power of the tongue. There is power in your words. How are you using the power you have in your tongue? Are you speaking words of truth into people's lives or words that are thoughtless? Sometimes it is hard for us to see our own weaknesses or know the harmful words we speak. I recommend finding a close family member, spouse, or a fellow believer you trust, and ask them for feedback to help you recognize any words you speak that are bringing harm, not life. Complete the two checklists below. The first checklist will help you recognize the areas where you are speaking unprofitable words. The second checklist will highlight areas where you are using your words to bless. Therefore, comparing these lists will help you see where you are either making wise word choices or where you need to recognize and change your word choices.

a.) Checklist: Speaking words that are unprofitable. (The more checkmarks you have, the more unprofitable words you are speaking.)

_____Do I often speak idle words about myself or others? Idle words are lazy, thoughtless, injurious, or unprofitable words?

_____Do I gossip which is to secretly attack another's character, or make murmurings like a snake charmer about someone (to entice others to join in on character assassination)?

_____Do I curse others or myself with my words? Examples: "I will never get better, and I will always be sick!" "You are about as dumb as they get!" "My life is a disaster, and it will never change!" "You will always be lacking in life!" "You will never get married!" "You will never succeed in life!"

_____Do I swear using the Lord's name in vain?

_____Do I frequently complain?

_____Do I speak words of death over myself or others? Example: "You will die young!"

_____When others speak words of death over themselves or others, am I agreeing with them?

_____Do I speak what someone wants to hear instead of the truth?

b.) Checklist: Profitable words. (The more checkmarks you have, the more you are using your words to bless.)

_____Do I use my words to confess Jesus as my Lord and Savior?

_____Do I bless myself, others, and God with my words?

_____Do I praise the LORD with my words often?

_____Do I use my words to decree a thing and it will be established? (Job 22:28)

_____Do I speak the word of God out loud since faith comes by hearing and hearing by the word of God?

_____Do I use my words to share Jesus with the lost?

_____Do I speak words that build up (bring life to people and situations)?

_____When others speak words of death or harm over themselves or others, am I using my words to cancel the lies and hurt spoken?

_____Do I use my words to resist Satan and renounce and rebuke his lies?

_____Do I use my words to pray and call things that are not as though they were?

_____Do I use my words to speak truth?

After examination of your words, what unprofitable word choices will you work to remove and replace with words that bless. The first step is to recognize your word choices, and then second, changing your mind about your unprofitable word choice. Third, devising an intentional plan to continue to recognize, stop, and replace your unprofitable words with words of life. For example: When I recognize I have spoken unprofitable words, I will say, "I cancel that." Therefore, I have acknowledged my poor word choice and recognize I need to make a correction. My next intentional step is to speak a word of life. This process is building a new habit of speaking profitable words. Journal below your intentional steps to build up (speak life) with your words and not tear down.

_____
_____
_____
_____
_____
_____
_____
_____
_____

_____
_____
_____
_____
_____
_____
_____
_____
_____

OUR SPIRITUAL AUTHORITY AS BELIEVERS, AND THE CHURCH

1. <u>Examining what you believe</u>: After reading Mark 16:15-20 in the King James Version, underline in pencil every time the word "believe" is written, circle each time the word "signs" is written, and draw a box around the words "shall" or "shall not." Meditate on these verses. Journal what you believe in your heart from these verses, then what you are struggling to believe. Ask God to teach and show you the truth from these verses. Everything we do as believers is to be done in faith, for it to produce the desired results. This includes using your authority as a believer in Jesus Christ.

_____
_____
_____
_____
_____
_____
_____
_____
_____
_____
_____
_____
_____
_____

2. <u>Part of recognizing your authority as a follower of Jesus Christ, is understanding your authority over Satan in your life</u>. You will examine this to ensure you understand the importance of removing Satan out of your life and out of your temple. Second Timothy 2:25-26 amplified states, *"He must correct those who are in opposition with courtesy and gentleness in the hope that God may grant that they will repent and be led to the knowledge of the truth [accurately understanding and welcoming it], and that they may come to their senses and escape from the trap of the devil, having been held captive by him to do his will."* The accuser of the brethren steals, kills, destroys, is cunning, deceptive, the father of lies, and powerfully aggressively fights against us. We must, therefore, resist Satan, and he will flee from us. To resist is to oppose. To oppose is to actively refuse to comply with his evil. He is a thief, and he will try to steal what is not his; and therefore, knowing how to stand and take your authority as a follower of Jesus Christ is essential.

<u>First, let's examine if Satan has gained access to your body, mind, or soul:</u> Do you recognize any areas of your body, mind, or soul where Satan has gained access to you? If so, have you closed the door where Satan got access by repenting and using your authority to resist and remove him from your life?

Do you feel oppression, heaviness, pressure, baggage, torment, constant irritation, are your emotions running your life, ruminating thoughts, etc. This is your life and your body, your mind, and your soul; use your authority as a believer in Jesus Christ and kick Satan out of your life. Journal the areas in your life where Satan has gained access, and journal your plan to take back your body, mind, and soul from the thief and the father of lies.

_____
_____
_____
_____
_____
_____
_____
_____
_____
_____
_____
_____
_____
_____
_____
_____

_____

_____

_____

_____

_____

_____

_____

OUR SPIRITUAL AUTHORITY: SPEAKING TO OUR MOUNTAIN

Understanding the King and His Kingdom (see page 80 of *Called to Truth, A Practical, Biblical Guide to Spiritual & Physical Wholeness*)

1. Who has access to the Keys of the Kingdom? Wouldn't it be someone who was part of the family? Read and journal your notes after reading Ephesians 2:19-22, Luke 12:32, and John 3:3-5.

_____

_____

_____

_____

_____

_____

_____

_____

_____

2. Since it is the LORD's will according to Matthew 6:9-10 that heaven be brought to earth, whose will are we waiting for? Study and journal your notes from: Genesis 1:26-28, Mark 16:15-20, and Acts 3:6-9.

_____

_____

_____

_____

_____

_____

_____

_____

_____

3. What are the Keys to the Kingdom of God? If keys open doors, what keys open the doors to God's Kingdom? How is heaven brought to earth? Study and journal your notes from the following scripture verses: Matthew 16:19, Matthew 18:18-20, and John 20:21-23. I encourage you to ask God to guide you into understanding the truths in these verses.

_____

_____

_____

_____

_____

_____

_____

_____

_____

_____

_____

_____

4. Journal your thoughts about this statement: There is a time to pray, and there is a time to use the authority God has given you. See Luke 10:19, Mark 16:17-18, Luke 13:12, and James 4:7.

_____

_____

_____

_____

_____

_____

_____

_____

_____

_____

_____

_____

_____

_____
_____
_____
_____
_____
_____
_____
_____
_____
_____
_____
_____
_____

⚓ Truth Basic Training Verses

Carefully study the following verses by reading the scripture in various translations, including the King James Version; underline any words that stand out to you; use a Strong's Concordance, which is an index of every word in the King James Version, and read the entire chapter of the verse. Journal your notes and summary.

"And Jesus came and spoke to them, saying, 'All power is given to Me in heaven and earth. Go you therefore, and teach all nations, baptizing them in the name of the Father, and of the Son, and of the Holy Ghost: Teaching them to observe all things whatsoever I have commanded you: and, lo, I am with you always even to the end of the world.' Amen." Matthew 28:18-20

_____
_____
_____
_____
_____
_____
_____
_____
_____

Your Journey to Truth

_____
_____
_____
_____
_____

CHAPTER 15

---❖---

SPIRITUAL WARFARE

FOR BY YOU HAVE I RUN THROUGH A TROOP: BY MY GOD HAVE I LEAPED OVER A WALL

Spiritual warfare can be fought in various ways. If you have not seen the 2015 movie, *War Room*, I suggest watching it to help you understand how you fight the spiritual battle. Our war against evil will be a confrontation in the physical realm and a confrontation in the spiritual realm. You will need to confront situations when they are extremely difficult and approach them God's way. You will not only be praying spiritual warfare prayers, but there will be times God leads us to speak truth and words of life to someone. A friend of mine kept repeating the same unhealthy behavior that was causing her harm. I was led to confront the evil in her mind that was deceiving her and telling her what she was doing had no negative consequences. I had to confront the situation in a truthful manner to shine the light on the darkness/lie in my friend's mind. The lie was harming her, and she was not able to recognize that at the time. The truth I spoke to her had to resonate louder than the lie, in order to drown out the lie she was believing. My motive was in love and my friend knew that and thus responded by recognizing the truth. Therefore, the lie had no more grip on her. In summary, my spiritual warfare prayers, using my authority to renounce and rebuke evil, in conjunction with speaking truth to my friend, dispelled the lies she was deceived into believing. Come along on **Your Journey to Truth** and put on the whole armor of God.

👣 YOUR JOURNEY TO TRUTH

After reading Chapter 15 of *Called to Truth, A Practical, Biblical Guide to Spiritual & Physical Wholeness*, what is spiritual warfare and why is it necessary?

_____

_____

_____

_____

_____

_____

_____

_____

_____

_____

_____

THE WHOLE ARMOR OF GOD

1. You will be able to stand against the schemes of the devil when you **"Put On the Whole Armor of God."** Name and describe each part of the Whole Armor of God (refer to pages 83-84 of *Called to Truth, A Practical, Biblical Guide to Spiritual & Physical Wholeness*:

_____

_____

_____

_____

_____

_____

_____

_____

_____

_____

_____

_____

_____

_____
_____
_____
_____
_____

2. All believers of Jesus Christ have a position in the body of Christ. You are to stand with your armor on and spiritually fight for God's truth to manifest on earth. You are vital to the body of Christ. You are to humbly follow His direction in taking your position. You can read and reflect on First Corinthians 12:12-31, Romans 12:4-21, and Ephesians 4:11-16. After reading and reflecting on these verses and statements, pray and seek the LORD about these truths for revelation. Journal your thoughts.

_____
_____
_____
_____
_____
_____
_____
_____
_____
_____
_____
_____
_____
_____
_____
_____
_____
_____
_____

SPIRITUAL WARFARE

1. After reading and studying page 85 of *Called to Truth, A Practical, Biblical Guide to Spiritual & Physical Wholeness*, write your own spiritual warfare prayers.

_____
_____
_____
_____
_____
_____
_____
_____
_____
_____
_____
_____
_____
_____
_____
_____
_____
_____
_____
_____
_____
_____
_____

2. As you are being armed with truth, where is God leading you to battle against the schemes of evil and defeat lies with truth?

_____
_____
_____
_____
_____
_____
_____
_____
_____
_____

3. Is there anyone God is leading you to pray for who is going through a spiritual battle right now? Are there any truths you have learned that could help them and that God is leading you to share with them?

_____

_____

_____

_____

_____

_____

_____

_____

_____

_____

4. While the world is speaking death, you will speak life to situations and bring them out of desolation and destruction. Write your spiritual warfare strategy to follow through with what God is calling you to do.

_____

_____

_____

_____

_____

_____

_____

_____

_____

_____

5. Speaking in tongues is a type of spiritual warfare. After you have received the baptism of the Holy Spirit, a sign that follows is speaking in tongues. When you are speaking in tongues, you are edifying (building up) yourself.

There was a day when I felt a lot of dark spiritual pressure around me. There was nothing specific going on that I could relate this to, therefore, I did not know how to pray. So I prayed in tongues at any opportunity I had, and it built up my spirit. Within a day, this pressure was gone from me. Refer to Chapter 18 of this study guide under the section *The Fullness of the Believer* and within that section you will find the *Baptism of the Holy Spirit*. If you have not received the baptism of the Holy Spirit and are interested in having a better understanding, I recommend reading that section.

⚓ Truth Basic Training Verses

Carefully study the following verses by reading the scripture in various translations, including the King James Version; underline any words that stand out to you; use a Strong's Concordance, which is an index of every word in the King James Version, and read the entire chapter of the verse. Journal your notes and summary.

"For by You I have run through a troop: by my God have I leaped over a wall." 2 Samuel 22:30

_____
_____
_____
_____
_____
_____
_____

"And from the days of John the Baptist until now the kingdom of heaven suffers violence, and the violent take it by force." Matthew 11:12

_____
_____
_____
_____
_____
_____
_____
_____

CHAPTER 16

SPIRITUAL CHECK-UP

As a young adult, I understood the value of hard work and never shied away from things that required persistence. Sometimes my efforts and striving would go too far and cause me stress. I thought my efforts could eventually solve whatever problem I had. I did not understand that I was supposed to turn my cares over to the LORD. It was like I heard and read scripture but had scales on the eyes of my heart and couldn't recognize truth. At the time, I did not have any revelation of how the word of God was alive and active. I did not have revelation that my faith would put into action the word of God.

I came to the knowledge of the truth and had revelation of God's spiritual principles/laws. One of the spiritual principles in Proverbs 3 is: trust in the LORD with all my heart, lean not on my own understanding, in all my ways acknowledge Him, and He will keep my path straight.

I was looking for answers in my own efforts and that is where I came up empty. I was supposed to trust God with all my heart, lean not on what I understood, acknowledge God in what I was doing, and He would then keep my path straight.

When I got to the end of my efforts and strength, I received revelation of His truth. I was to seek Him with all my heart and when I started seeking Him for my answers and not the resources of the world, my peace came flooding in. I was seeking all the world's resources and not even looking at what the word of God said. I had been stuck for many years in the same place spiritually. I had not grown spiritually in my faith for decades. I was not even aware that I should be moving from glory to glory. I was spiritually stuck in the mud. I had to come to the realization that when I would seek God with

all my heart, I would find Him and find my peace and joy. Likewise, when you seek God with **all your heart**, you will find Him and His truth! I had to look outside the walls of containment that the world and Satan tried to entangle me with, and instead, seek His truth above all else. Others unknowingly can try to contain you in a box of what is comfortable for them. However, if you truly want to run your race well, you will seek Him with all your heart and not follow the fairy tales of this world. Come along on **Your Journey to Truth** in seeking God with all your heart.

👣 YOUR JOURNEY TO TRUTH

<u>SPIRITUAL CHECK-UP QUESTIONS:</u>

After reading Chapter 16 of *Called to Truth, A Practical, Biblical Guide to Spiritual & Physical Wholeness* and after **praying**, ask the LORD to reveal to you any stumbling blocks in your life. The following questions are a tool to help you test and evaluate your spiritual condition.

Check-up question 1: Journal below the areas of your life that you have freedom and the areas you are struggling to gain freedom.

I have freedom and am following the LORD in these areas of my life:

_____
_____
_____
_____
_____
_____
_____
_____
_____
_____
_____

I am struggling in these areas of my life to find my peace, joy, and freedom (a trusted family member or friend can give insight):

_____
_____
_____
_____
_____
_____

_____
_____
_____
_____

Check-up question 2: Have you grown in your walk with the Lord or are you still at the place you began years ago?

_____
_____
_____
_____
_____
_____
_____

Below are questions to evaluate your journey of faith and record your growth, your steps backwards, or if no steps have been made. You are to move from glory to glory, and if no movement has been made it is time to evaluate why.

List the areas you have grown in your faith walk.

_____
_____
_____
_____
_____
_____
_____
_____
_____
_____
_____

List any areas in your life where you may have backslid and evaluate why this happened.

_____
_____
_____
_____
_____
_____
_____
_____

Has my faith walk been stagnant for a long time and why?

_____
_____
_____
_____
_____
_____
_____

Check-up question 3: Calculate the estimated amount of time you spend daily seeking truth from the word of God and praying. Time spent:

_____

Calculate the estimated amount of time you spend daily seeking news and information from the world, news sources, social media, etc. Time spent:

_____

Journal your observations about how much time you spend seeking truth from God versus seeking news and information from the world.

_____
_____
_____
_____
_____
_____

Check-up question 4: Now is the time to ask God to reveal to you any strongholds in your thinking or lies that have crept into your life. A stronghold in your thinking is a fortress that has been built up to protect a lie or sin. If you have a fellow believer you trust, you can ask for their help. Sometimes, someone we know closely can detect evil working through us that we can't see for ourselves. The sooner we expose Satan's deceptions in our lives, the sooner we can get free. Be careful not to get offended by someone telling you the truth that can save your life. Journal any lies that have been exposed or any strongholds in your thinking. The goal is to expose the lie and thus weaken the hold it has on you and cast it out of your life.

_____

_____

_____

_____

_____

_____

_____

_____

_____

_____

_____

_____

_____

_____

_____

_____

_____

_____

_____

_____

_____

Check-up question 5: After examining your spirit, place a check mark next to the fruit of the Spirit that your spirit displays regularly and leave blank the fruit of the Spirit that is not displayed very often.

_____ Love (unselfish concern for others, good will, brotherly love)

_____ Joy (Romans 15:13, *Now the God of hope fill you with all joy and peace in believing, that you may abound in hope, through the power of the Holy Spirit.*)

_____ Peace (assurance, secure)

_____ Long-suffering (patience, endurance)

_____ Gentleness (integrity, virtuous, speaking truth with gentleness)

_____ Goodness (upright in heart and in life, benevolence)

_____ Faith (persuasion, belief that prevails)

_____ Meekness (not weakness but exercising God's strength under His control)

_____ Temperance (self-control)

(Galatians 5:22-23 KJV)

When we Walk in the Spirit, we will not fulfill the lusts of the flesh. The works of the flesh go against the Spirit. If we live in the Spirit, the word of God says, "let us also walk in the Spirit." According to Galatians 5:19-21, evidence of the works of the flesh are adultery, fornication, uncleanness, lasciviousness (sensuality), idolatry, witchcraft, hatred, variance (discord), emulations (jealousy), wrath, strife, seditions (dissensions), heresies, envy, murders, drunkenness, and reveling.

Is the Holy Spirit leading you to any works of the flesh (those listed above) that you need to rebuke and renounce out of your life? These lusts of the flesh go against or fight against walking in the Spirit. Journal what has been revealed to you from the fruit of the Spirit checklist and from the list of the lusts of the flesh.

_____
_____
_____
_____
_____
_____
_____
_____
_____
_____
_____

Check-up question 6: According to Habakkuk 2:2-3, _"And the LORD answered me, and said, 'Write the vision, and make it plain upon tables, that he may run that read it. For the vision is yet for an appointed time, but at the end it shall speak, and not lie: though it tarry, wait for it; because it will surely come, it will not tarry.'"_ Writing a vision for your life is a biblical principle.

Molly Seidel won the bronze medal in the women's Olympic marathon in the 2020 Summer Olympics. When she was in fourth grade, she wrote down on a piece of paper: _"I wish I will make it into the Olympics and win a gold medal."_ This was only the third marathon she had ever run. As the age of 27, Molly won her Olympic medal, and the vision she wrote down in fourth grade came to pass.

My family and I watched the marathon on television and saw Molly win the bronze medal. The excitement was in the air as we heard the crowd cheering her on and saw the passion and drive in Molly as she finished the race. Shortly after the marathon aired, they showed the note Molly wrote in fourth grade that she was going to be in the Olympics and win a medal. Writing out a vision for your life gives you a goal to work towards and a plan you can commit to the LORD for His direction.

Are you seeking the LORD's plan for your life? Do you know the vision God has for your life or are you not sure? If you are unsure about the plans God has for your life, pray and ask Him. Write out a vision for your life and the steps to achieve the goals God has put in your heart. Commit your plans to the LORD according to Proverbs 3:5-6.

_____

_____

_____

_____

_____

_____

_____

_____

_____

_____

_____

_____

_____

_____

_____

_____

_____

_____

_____

_____

_____

_____

_____

_____

_____

_____
_____
_____
_____

Check-up question 7: After reading and studying page 88 of _Called to Truth, A Practical, Biblical Guide to Spiritual & Physical Wholeness_ and the listed scripture verses of First Timothy 4:1-7, **journal the signs of deception in the latter days**:

_____
_____
_____
_____
_____
_____
_____
_____
_____

Check-up question 8: Signs of Pride

Now you will examine your heart for signs of pride referenced on page 88 and 89 of "_Called to Truth, A Practical, Biblical Guide to Spiritual & Physical Wholeness_". Pride is arrogance, haughtiness, looks down on others, self-exaltation, self-absorption, or puffed up. There can be various ranges of pride. It is much easier to stop pride or any other sin, in the early stages, before it grows into a deeply rooted sin of pride. Record your answers to the following questions:

1. Do you easily find fault in others and not yourself?

_____
_____
_____

2. Are you defensive?

_____
_____
_____

3. Are you too concerned with how others perceive you?

_____
_____
_____
_____

4. Do you have a high need for attention and praise?

_____
_____
_____

If you answered yes to any or all these questions, ask the LORD to lead you into humility. Proverbs 11:2 says, *"When pride comes, then comes shame; but with the lowly (humble) is wisdom."* Proverbs 22:4 says, *"By humility and the fear of the LORD are riches, and honor, and life."*

Check-up question 9: Comparing Yourself to Others

If you tend to compare yourself with others, refer to page 89 of *Called to Truth, A Practical, Biblical Guide to Spiritual & Physical Wholeness*. Journal below whom you compare yourself to and recognize that it is a pitfall. Journal your plan to recognize and stop comparing yourself to others. Galatians 6:4 says, *"But let every man prove his own work, and then shall he have rejoicing in himself alone, and not in another."*

_____
_____
_____
_____
_____
_____
_____
_____
_____
_____

Check-up question 10: Examining your Thoughts

Journal the top five things you spend your time thinking about (refer to page 89 of *Called to Truth, A Practical, Biblical Guide to Spiritual & Physical Wholeness*). Next to each, determine what fruit your thought produces. For example: if one of your top five thoughts was worry, the fruit it produces is unhealthy emotion which can lead to physical problems and making poor decisions. Second example: if God is not in my top priority of thoughts, what fruit can that produce? If God is not my priority, I can easily be deceived and have very little or no good fruit in my life. My life would become meaningless.

1. _____
   _____
   _____
   _____
   _____

2. _____
   _____
   _____
   _____
   _____

3. _____
   _____
   _____
   _____
   _____

4. _____
   _____
   _____
   _____
   _____

5. _____
   _____
   _____
   _____
   _____

Check-up question 11: Making God Pleasing Decisions

In reference to page 90 of *Called to Truth, A Practical, Biblical Guide to Spiritual & Physical Wholeness*, summarize below the steps you will take to make God pleasing decisions.

_____
_____

In summary, the above Spiritual Check-up evaluation, is to help you first recognize lies, strongholds, sin, disobedience, and backwardness. Second, it is to weaken the lies, strongholds, sin, disobedience, and backwardness by receiving truth and thus cast them out of your life. Furthermore, it is to recognize areas in your life that are spiritually prospering and to continue to nurture those areas spiritually.

⚓ Truth Basic Training Verses

Carefully study the following verses by reading the scripture in various translations, including the King James Version; underline any words that stand out to you; use a Strong's Concordance, which is an index of every word in the King James Version, and read the entire chapter of the verse. Journal your notes and summary.

"Test and evaluate yourselves to see whether you are in the faith and living your lives as [committed] believers. Examine yourselves [not me]! Or do you not recognize this about yourselves [by an ongoing experience] that Jesus Christ is in you, unless indeed you fail the test and are rejected as counterfeit?" Second Corinthians 13:5 (Amplified)

CHAPTER 17

WE CHOOSE

One of the biggest lies with which Satan tricked me was that I had no choices. Satan caged me up with his lies that I had to break free from. Your mind is one of your biggest assets because you control your mind. Satan wants to control it, but you have control to cut off evil imaginations and cast off the lies that Satan tries to place there. We need to be diligent and quickly cast out evil thoughts before a pathway has been worn down in our mind.

Another very important choice we make is our words. A valuable plan I put into action was an intentional strategy plan. It was important for me to recognize idle words that I spoke and idle words others spoke. If I caught myself speaking an idle word, I would correct myself. Idle words are words that are empty, fruitless, useless, unprofitable, barren, lazy, foolish, careless, and inactive. The word of God says you are accountable for every idle word spoken. Sometimes, we just go along with other's comments made in ignorance, but we have power in our choices. Agreeing with idle words has power, and I recognized the power of whose words I agreed with or was being passive about. In addition, if someone starts cursing their life with their words, it is important not to agree with their words. When you start paying close attention to your words and others', you will recognize the amount of useless and careless talk there is. Come along on **Your Journey to Truth** in recognizing the importance of your choices.

👣 YOUR JOURNEY TO TRUTH

YOU CHOOSE: I HAVE SET BEFORE YOU LIFE AND DEATH, BLESSING AND CURSING

God does not manipulate anyone. He created man in His image. You have a free will to choose. The angels have free will and Lucifer chose pride. According to Isaiah 14:12-14, *"How art thou fallen from heaven, O Lucifer, son of the morning! How art thou cut down to the ground, which didst weaken the nations! For thou hast said in thine heart, I will ascend into heaven, I will exalt my throne above the stars of God: I will sit also upon the mount of the congregation, in the sides of the north: I will ascend above the heights of the clouds: I will be like the Most High."* These verses show his will in choosing to put himself above God; and therefore, was thrown out of heaven. In Genesis Chapter 3, we all know the choice Adam and Eve made in the Garden of Eden after falling for the subtle lies of the serpent.

1. Satan will try to steal your choices. He wants to steal your ability to choose and will try to do that any way he can. Satan will manipulate you into thinking you don't have a choice. I can testify to this because Satan had deceived me into believing I had no choices. After reading Chapter 17 of *Called to Truth, A Practical, Biblical Guide to Spiritual & Physical Wholeness*, list some areas where you make choices.

_____

_____

_____

_____

_____

_____

_____

_____

_____

_____

_____

_____

2. It is important to **evaluate/test your choices.** Sometimes, by not making a choice you are making a choice, because if you are not intentionally making decisions and choices, time will make the decisions/choices for you. Therefore, let's review some areas of your life to test your choices.

a.) What choices am I making about <u>spending time with God in prayer and studying the word of God</u>? Journal what your current plan is, determine if a change needs to be made, and write out your new plan.

_____

_____

_____

_____

_____

_____

_____

_____

b.) <u>Relationship choices</u>:

What choices am I currently making in my relationships? Who am I choosing to spend my time with?

_____

_____

_____

_____

_____

_____

_____

_____

What relationships are impacting me in a positive or negative way?

_____

_____

_____

_____

_____

_____

_____

_____

_____

What is my plan for spending time with the important people in my life?

_____
_____
_____
_____
_____
_____
_____

What is my plan to intentionally bless others?

_____
_____
_____
_____
_____
_____

c.) <u>Mind, will, and emotions:</u>

What do I choose to spend my time meditating on and imagining?

_____
_____
_____
_____

Am I making choices to guard my heart and emotions?

_____
_____
_____
_____
_____
_____
_____

Am I being intentional with my free will and not being controlled or manipulated?

_____
_____

_____

_____

_____

_____

_____

I would like to share with you an example of being intentional in guarding your heart. Early on in my life, I knew I wanted to be a mom one day. I loved children and being around them brought me immense joy. The sound of a child's laughter was beautiful, joyous music to my soul. I had a miscarriage about four years after being married. My heart had longed for a baby. The loss was devastating to me. I had an empty feeling inside of me. My womb was carrying a baby and now it was empty, and I felt the emptiness. I had never even thought about the possibility of a miscarriage. The baby was to be in my womb 40 weeks not 14, and I could feel the loss. I felt in my heart she was a little baby girl. I had never processed through the pain or loss of this. I never talked about it to anyone or even prayed about it, but almost hid it away in my heart. Quite recently, the LORD drew me to pray about the healing of my heart from the pain of losing a baby from a miscarriage. I never even realized I was holding pain in my heart from this loss because it had been many years ago. Time does not automatically heal a wound, but Jesus heals our wounds. I invited the LORD in to heal my heart, and I released the pain. It was a beautiful exchange of love that day when I released the pain of my miscarriage and asked the LORD to heal my heartache. After praying and releasing the pain, I felt lighter on the inside and received the love of Jesus to heal the emptiness from the loss of that child. After the miscarriage, I went on to have two wonderful children and treasure their laughter and lives. The Lord is waiting for you to come to Him to heal whatever is hurting or hidden!

Journal your plan to be intentional with your mind, will, and emotions. How will you be intentional about your thoughts and imagination, about guarding your heart and emotions, and about your choices and free will?

_____

_____

_____

_____

_____

_____

_____

_____

_____

_____

d.) <u>Choices for my future</u>:

What traits and gifts has God created you with? In planning for your future, how will you consider the unique way God created you in the planning of your future?

_____

_____

_____

_____

_____

_____

_____

_____

_____

_____

_____

_____

_____

Have I prayed to God about my future?

_____

_____

Do I have wise people, in my life, I can seek for godly wisdom for my future?

_____

_____

Am I following biblical principles in making decisions for my future? Proverbs is a great book of the Bible for wisdom. Journal biblical principles you will use to make decisions for your future.

_____

_____

_____

_____

_____

_____

_____

Am I at peace with the choices I have made for my future? Why and why not? If not, keep seeking God and His word for wisdom.

_____

_____

_____

_____

_____

_____

_____

_____

TRIALS AND TEMPTATIONS

After reading page 95 of *Called to Truth, A Practical, Biblical Guide to Spiritual & Physical Wholeness*, what points are important to remember when you are <u>facing trials and temptations.</u>

1. _____

_____

2. _____

_____

3. _____

_____

4. _____

_____

⚓ Truth Basic Training Verses

Carefully study the following verses by reading the scripture in various translations, including the King James Version; underline any words that stand out to you; use a Strong's Concordance, which is an index of every word in the King James Version, and read the entire chapter of the verse. Journal your notes and summary.

"I call heaven and earth to record this day against you, that I have set before you life and death, blessing and cursing: therefore choose life, that both you and your seed may live."
Deut. 30:19

_____

_____

_____

_____

_____

_____

"And if it seem evil to you to serve the LORD, choose you this day whom you will serve; whether the gods which your fathers served that were on the other side of the flood, or the gods of the Amorites in whose land you dwell: but as for me and my house, we will serve the LORD." Joshua 24:15

_____

_____

_____

_____

_____

CHAPTER 18

GOD'S HOSPITAL: HEALING, DELIVERANCE, AND WHOLENESS

The Very God of Peace Sanctify You Wholly

What does it mean to be whole? "Wholly" (see First Thessalonians 5:23, King James Version) is to be complete, perfect, whole, entire sanctification, and unbroken. Our God is a God of peace and wants peace in your body, mind, soul, and spirit.

Quite a few years ago, I had a lot of pain in my muscles and joints and noticed my breathing was shallow. I had some physical therapy for carpal tunnel syndrome and had other arthritic pain. I relieved some of my pain by walking and exercising. After coming to the knowledge of the truth that God was my Healer and I am to seek Him, I recognized that I had been trained for years by anxiety and fear. I had learned bad habits of worrying, and this unhealthy behavior had consequences to my body. God's word says to cast your cares to Him, and when I didn't follow His direction, there were consequences to my body. God had not given me a spirit of fear. The spirit of fear was from Satan, and it had trained my body for years. Once I came out of that agreement, my body was healed! God and His word became by trainer; fear was no longer by trainer. God has given me a spirit of power, love, and sound mind through His healing scriptures and the Holy Spirit! Come along on **Your Journey to Truth** to God's healing, deliverance, and wholeness for your life.

👣 YOUR JOURNEY TO TRUTH

Before moving onto this section of our study, carefully read Chapter 18 of *Called to Truth, A Practical, Biblical Guide to Spiritual & Physical Wholeness*.

HEALING – GOD'S HOSPITAL, pages 98-101 of *Called to Truth, A Practical, Biblical Guide to Spiritual & Physical Wholeness*.

If you have not come to the revelation of God's healing power or that He wants you well, I recommend reading Chapter 18 out loud and praying to God for revelation. Faith comes by hearing, and this chapter is packed with scriptures on healing and revelatory truth.

1. Let's pretend for the sake of this question that you are in a court of law, and you will bring forth evidence that God is a good God and wants you healed and whole. Journal the evidence (from this chapter and scripture) to prove your case.

_____
_____
_____
_____
_____
_____
_____
_____
_____
_____
_____
_____
_____
_____
_____
_____
_____
_____

2. <u>God has a spiritual order to His creation</u>. When there is disorder in our family; disorder in our marriage; disorder in our job; disorder in our mind; disorder in our heart; disorder in our body; and/or disorder in our spirit, something has moved out of His divine order. If there is anything out of order in your life from the above list or any other areas, list those areas of your life where you need God to restore order. Then determine one

intentional step you can take to bring your life back in order according to God's truth.

_____

_____

_____

_____

_____

_____

_____

_____

_____

_____

3. Let's review a scripture that helps <u>explain a spiritual law/principle of God's Kingdom</u>. God speaks in Exodus 15:26, "*If you will diligently hearken to the voice of the LORD your God, and will do that which is right in His sight, and will give ear to His commandments, and keep all His statutes, I will put none of these diseases upon you, which I have brought upon the Egyptians: for I am the LORD that heals you.*"

Let's examine this above verse. Underline the word "will" in this verse. There was a decision to be made. They chose with their "will" whether they would listen to the LORD, do what was right in God's sight, and hear and keep His laws. The Bible is full of spiritual principles and laws that operate in the spiritual realm. For example: If you do not honor your parents, there is a curse that comes. Deuteronomy 27:16 says, "*Cursed be he that dishonors his father or his mother. And all the people shall say, Amen.*" There are many other verses that speak of the spiritual law of dishonoring your mother and father: Leviticus 20:9, Matthew 15:4, Exodus 21:15, 17, Proverbs 20:20, Exodus 20:12, Deuteronomy 21:18-21, and Mark 7:9-13.

Explore the scripture and journal one spiritual law/principle to help build your understanding of this. When you are searching the Bible for a spiritual law/principle, you are looking for a spiritual law/principle that applies to the followers of Jesus today. Thereby, the religious rules for the priests for the nation of Israel in Leviticus would not be a law/principle for a follower of Jesus today. One suggestion would be to search the book of Proverbs for a spiritual law/principle.

_____

_____

_____

_____
_____
_____
_____
_____
_____
_____
_____
_____

4. After reading pages 98 – 101 of *Called to Truth, A Practical, Biblical Guide to Spiritual & Physical Wholeness*, journal how the word of God is healing medicine. Give examples in scripture.

_____
_____
_____
_____
_____
_____
_____
_____
_____
_____

5. Let's examine a statement I made on page 99 of *Called to Truth, A Practical, Biblical Guide to Spiritual & Physical Wholeness*: "Shouldn't we suffer for the truth, not a lie of the enemy?" Let's look at First Peter 4:19 which says, *"Therefore let those who suffer according to the will of God commit their souls to Him in doing good as to a faithful Creator."* Additionally, Second Timothy 3:12 says if we live a godly life, we will suffer persecution. The world will not understand or accept our ways as followers of Jesus Christ. You are called to bring heaven to earth. You are called to be truth seekers and truth speakers. You are His ambassadors doing His work on the earth. Jesus taught the truth when He encountered those in need and did not withhold His kingdom gifts of healing and deliverance from them. Following the principles of Jesus will not be accepted by some, and we will endure suffering.

But you don't want to be suffering for something that is a lie. For example, if Satan has convinced you that God wants you to stay sick and that when you continue to suffer with disease and sickness it is a good thing, doesn't this go against God's name of "Jehovah Rapha, The God Who Heals?" If you are under oppression from Satan, doesn't God want you to be delivered since He is the Deliverer? Journal your thoughts on these last two paragraphs and both underlined statements.

_____

_____

_____

_____

_____

_____

_____

_____

6. Journal your thoughts about the following statement: It is important for a person who needs healing to understand that God wants them well.

_____

_____

_____

_____

_____

_____

_____

7. After reading about the importance of forgiveness and the medical evidence on page 99 of *Called to Truth, A Practical, Biblical Guide to Spiritual & Physical Wholeness*, what are the physical consequences of unforgiveness and what are the spiritual consequences of unforgiveness? See Matthew 6:14-15.

_____

_____

_____

_____

_____

_____

_____

8. Refer to pages 99 – 100 of *Called to Truth, A Practical, Biblical Guide to Spiritual & Physical Wholeness*, answer the eight questions on the lines below from page 100 to help determine if there is a possible correlation between a physical sickness and a soul wound (unhealed soul):

TEST THE HEALTH OF YOUR SOUL

1) Is the Holy Spirit bringing anything to your attention that you need to deal with or repent of?

_____
_____
_____
_____

2) Are you harboring unforgiveness towards someone, towards yourself, or towards God?

_____
_____
_____
_____

If you have not forgiven someone, read page 16-17, 22-24, 29-31, and 58-60 of *Called to Truth, A Practical, Biblical Guide to Spiritual & Physical Wholeness* and the scripture verses within these pages. Pray to your Heavenly Father and seek Him with your whole heart about the issue. Journal your notes on forgiveness on the lines below.

_____
_____
_____
_____
_____
_____
_____
_____

3) Are you engaging in repetitive sin that you refuse to remove from your life?

_____
_____
_____
_____

Repentance refers to when you have a change of mind and you recognize your wrong thinking. You can refer to page 16-17, 21-24, 30-31, 58-61 of *Called to Truth, A Practical, Biblical Guide to Spiritual & Physical Wholeness* for truths on repentance. When you come to the LORD with your whole heart and repent (a change of mind), He will lead you into freedom from the bondage of sin.

We all sin and fall short of the glory of God. But as followers of Jesus Christ, you move from glory to glory; the process of sanctification occurs as you follow Him humbly and obediently. Therefore, you will not be practicing sinning. If you are struggling with a repetitive sin, fasting according to Isaiah 58 will loose the bands of wickedness, undo the heavy burden, let the oppressed go free, and break every yoke. Jeremiah 29:13 says, *"Any you shall seek Me and find Me, when you shall search for Me with all your heart."* When you come humbly to God in this way, He will show you the way to freedom! Journal your notes on repentance and repetitive sin on the lines below.

_____
_____
_____
_____
_____
_____
_____
_____
_____

4) Do you love God, yourself, and others?

_____
_____
_____
_____

If you have recognized you have been unloving towards yourself, God, or another person, read and meditate on First Corinthians 13:4-7 and Matthew 22:37-40. Journal your notes on the lines below.

_____
_____
_____
_____

5) Does fear reside in your life?

_____
_____
_____
_____

If you have recognized the presence of fear in your life, you can review page 18 and pages 44-45 of *Called to Truth, A Practical, Biblical Guide to Spiritual & Physical Wholeness* and meditate on the scriptures within these pages. Second Timothy 1:7 states, *"For God has not given us the spirit of fear; but of power, and of love, and of a sound mind."* If fear is running your life, it is likely a spirit of fear has invaded. You will need to recognize fear in your life, repent for agreeing with fear, stand on the word of God, and cast fear out of your life. Journal your notes on the lines below.

_____
_____
_____
_____
_____
_____
_____
_____
_____
_____

6) Test your thoughts and heart with the Word of God. Are any of your thoughts contrary to the Word of God? Do you have wrong thinking patterns? Ask someone you trust to help you examine this.

_____
_____
_____
_____
_____
_____
_____
_____

If you have recognized your thinking has gone astray from the truth, Romans 12:2 says, *"And be not conformed to this world: but be you transformed by the renewing of your mind, that you may prove what is that good, and acceptable, and perfect, will of God."* It would be important to examine your life and the areas where you are conforming to the world's ways and not what God says. A good starting point would be to begin each day with reading the Bible and praying. If you have been listening to Satan's lies for quite a while, it is quite possible you have a stronghold in your thinking and possible demonic oppression. I would recommend reading and meditating on Second Corinthians 10:3-5. It is imperative to read scripture out loud and often to renew your mind with God's word. Be patient as the word of God transforms your thinking. Begin to purposefully start acknowledging when lies from Satan come into your mind and cast them off, and then read scripture out loud. When dark thoughts come in, try clapping your hands loud to snap off the thought. Begin the practice of casting off evil imaginations and begin imagining God's healing and His beautiful love for you. Journal your notes on the lines below.

_____
_____
_____
_____
_____
_____
_____
_____
_____
_____
_____
_____
_____
_____
_____
_____
_____
_____

7) Is your soul wounded (unhealed soul)? Are you holding on to past pain, regret, etc.?

_____
_____
_____
_____

8) Do you have shame or guilt that you haven't released?

_____
_____
_____
_____

If you have recognized you are holding onto pain, hurt, regret, shame, or guilt and are ready to release it from your soul: First, recognize and speak the truth about the pain, hurt, regret, shame, or guilt without rehearsing it but acknowledging the truth about the situation. Journal your notes below:

_____
_____
_____
_____
_____
_____
_____
_____
_____
_____
_____
_____

Second, if there is anyone you have not forgiven, including yourself, when you are ready to release this to God: (a) repent, which is a change of mind, recognize your healing comes when you release the cares of this world to God, and obey His word, and (b) confess with your mouth and release out of your belly the pain and any person you may have been holding onto in your soul. Journal your confession to God of releasing the pain and the situation to God and receive His healing touch.

_____
_____
_____
_____
_____
_____
_____
_____
_____
_____

Last, pray that through the completed work of Jesus Christ and the healing power of the Holy Spirit, you are healed. Journal your notes on the lines below.

_____
_____
_____
_____
_____

_____

_____

In summary of the above eight questions under TEST THE HEALTH OF YOUR SOUL, if you have recognized an area in your soul that needs healing, the following are steps to move you towards your healing:

1. Journal what soul issues have been recognized from the eight questions under TEST THE HEALTH OF YOUR SOUL. Be specific and acknowledge the truth that has been revealed to you in the lines below.

_____
_____
_____
_____
_____
_____
_____
_____

2. If the LORD has led you to repentance (a change of mind) about an issue you have recognized in the above eight questions under TEST THE HEALTH OF YOUR SOUL, journal below the truth He has revealed to you.

_____
_____
_____
_____

3. Confess with your mouth and release out of your belly any pain, hurt, lies, sin, person, or situation that you are casting out and no longer holding on to. Journal your confession to God of releasing the pain and situation to Him and receiving His hand of healing and deliverance. Receive the love of God for your healing and the power of the Holy Spirit to restore your soul. The LORD wants to heal your innermost parts and loves you dearly! Receive His love in your innermost parts. (Psalm 139:13-16 Amplified)

_____
_____
_____
_____
_____

_____
_____
_____
_____
_____
_____

If you have a physical illness not related to a soul wound (unhealed soul), you can read healing scriptures out loud, lay hands on yourself daily, and pray that God leads you to the next step for your healing. Your faith is important during this process, therefore, continue to rebuke doubt and unbelief and kick it out of your life. Be patient during this process, the important thing is to know the truth that God is your Healer. To pursue truth, pursue Him. Pursuing the LORD is the most important thing in your journey. When you abide in Him, you will have what you need.

DELIVERANCE – GOD'S HOSPITAL, pages 101-107 of "_Called to Truth, A Practical, Biblical Guide to Spiritual & Physical Wholeness_".

1. What is deliverance?

_____
_____
_____
_____

2. How did Jesus overcome Satan?

_____
_____
_____

3. What does it mean to overcome?

_____
_____
_____
_____

4. Who are you to overcome, and how do you overcome?

_____
_____

_____

_____

TEST YOURSELF: Has Satan gained any ground in your life? The details of the below questions are explained on pages 102-103 of _Called to Truth, A Practical, Biblical Guide to Spiritual & Physical Wholeness_.

1. Are you willfully sinning which is practicing to sin? Do I live a life of repentance?

_____

_____

_____

_____

_____

2. Pray and ask God to reveal any lies you may be believing. Anyone can be deceived, and thus we need to be vigilant. There is a list to help you detect deceptions and lies on pages 8-9 of _Called to Truth, A Practical, Biblical Guide to Spiritual & Physical Wholeness_.

_____

_____

_____

_____

3. Is your soul anchored in anything other than God (what direction is your soul drawing you to)?

_____

_____

_____

_____

_____

4. Are you putting someone or something above God in your life (what and who do you worship)?

_____

_____

_____

_____

_____

5. Are you grounded in truth?

_____
_____
_____
_____
_____

6. Are you oppressed with an evil spirit (signs: being enticed to do things you don't want to do; addictions; feelings of being tortured; ruminating thoughts that you don't want; feelings of being enslaved; feeling like you have extra baggage on your body you can't get rid of; feeling like you are under pressure and thus putting that pressure on others; attack of the mind, body, or soul, etc.)?

_____
_____
_____
_____
_____

7. Do you have any strongholds in your mind (a fortress built up in your mind to believe something that is holding you back from the truth)? I suggest you find someone you trust to help you examine whether there is a stronghold in your mind because this will be hard to detect yourself.

_____
_____
_____
_____
_____
_____
_____

8. Are you cursing yourself or others with your words?

_____
_____
_____
_____

9. If you have determined you have a soul wound (unhealed soul), journal whatever truth has been revealed to you about this. Refer to the above section of this study guide in Chapter 18, under TEST THE HEALTH OF YOUR SOUL and answer the eight questions if you haven't completed them yet.

_____

_____

_____

_____

_____

_____

_____

If you have recognized from your answers to these nine questions of TEST YOURSELF that Satan has gained ground or territory in your life, complete the below a, b, c, and d points:

a.) Journal the scripture verses that have brought revelation. (Refer to scripture verses listed on pages 102-103 of "*Called to Truth, A Practical, Biblical Guide to Spiritual & Physical Wholeness*".)

_____

_____

_____

_____

b.) Journal the lie, sin, or problem that has been exposed.

_____

_____

_____

_____

_____

c.) Journal the scripture you will meditate on to weaken the oppression (lie, evil invasion). Search scripture for a verse that builds truth in your heart for the lie or sin you are casting out of your life.

_____

_____

_____

_____

_____

d.) Journal your declarations to cast out the lie or sin.

_____

_____

_____

_____

_____

_____

_____

DELIVERANCE AND EVIL SPIRITS (DEMONS)

1. According to James 4:7-10, how do you get Satan to flee (run away) from you?

_____

_____

_____

_____

_____

_____

_____

_____

2. List the weapons of our warfare to fight Satan according to Second Corinthians 10:4-5.

_____

_____

_____

_____

_____

3. How do you confront evil in the spiritual realm, and how do you confront evil in the physical realm? (Refer to page 105 of _Called to Truth, A Practical, Biblical Guide to Spiritual & Physical Wholeness._)

_____

_____

_____

_____

_____

EVIL SPIRITS (DEMONS)

1. We will now take a moment to examine Ephesians 6:12 before we move onto the next question. We do not wrestle or struggle with human beings, but against the spiritual kingdom led by Satan. Satan has a spiritual kingdom that is outlined in this verse: principalities, powers, rulers of the darkness of this world, and spiritual wickedness in high places. There are spiritual principalities that rule regions, there are spiritual powers we do not see with our physical eye, there are evil spiritual rulers leading this world, and there is spiritual wickedness in high places. The lowest level of Satan's kingdom is demonic, and listed on page 106 are many of the verses in the Bible speaking of the demonic spiritual realm. We can be influenced by the demonic realm working through someone else that may oppress us because of the manifestations of evil working through them. Those that are believers of Jesus Christ have the Holy Spirit residing in their spirit. Therefore, believers cannot have demons in their spirit but can be infected with a demon or demons in their body, mind, or soul. List below some of the demons spoken about in scripture and listed on page 106 of *Called to Truth, A Practical, Biblical Guide to Spiritual & Physical Wholeness.*

_____

_____

_____

_____

_____

_____

_____

_____

_____

_____

2. What signs will there be that someone is oppressed with demonic influence? (See page 106 of *Called to Truth, A Practical, Biblical Guide to Spiritual & Physical Wholeness.*) List some scripture verses that speak of this truth.

_____

_____

_____

_____

_____

_____

3. What are some of the ways demonic influence can be removed/cast out of your life? (See page 106 and 107 of _Called to Truth, A Practical, Biblical Guide to Spiritual & Physical Wholeness._)

_____

_____

_____

_____

C.) <u>OUR WHOLENESS – GOD'S HOSPITAL</u>, pages 108-116 of _Called to Truth, A Practical, Biblical Guide to Spiritual & Physical Wholeness._

Journal the words of First Thessalonians 5:23-24 and look-up the definitions of sanctify and wholly and record them below.

_____

_____

_____

_____

1. <u>BODY</u>: After reading First Corinthians 6:13-20, what sin is against your own body? _____ According to verse 19, your body is the temple of who? _____ What does it mean in verse 20 when it says, "for you are bought with a price." See Acts 20:28.

_____

_____

_____

How are you to glorify God in your body and in your spirit which are God's?

_____

_____

_____

_____

_____

Your Journey to Truth

2. INNER MAN: spirit, soul, mind, and conscience.

a.) **Your Spirit**: According to John 14:16-19, how is the believer's spirit different from the unbeliever's spirit?

_____

_____

_____

_____

_____

According to Romans 8:11, what is the work of the Holy Spirit that dwells within us?

_____

_____

_____

_____

b.) **Your Soul**: After reading page 108-109 of _Called to Truth, A Practical, Biblical Guide to Spiritual & Physical Wholeness_ on the soul, what is the soul? Explain the choice you make regarding what you listen to.

_____

_____

_____

_____

_____

Why are you to diligently keep, guard, and watch over your heart according to Proverbs 4:23 and 3 John 2?

_____

_____

_____

_____

If a person has a wounded soul (unhealed pain/hurt), what are they more likely to listen to? (Page 110)

_____

_____

_____
_____

c.) <u>Your Mind</u>: Who decides what imaginations and thoughts you meditate on? Therefore, how do you filter your thoughts according to Second Corinthians 10:5?

_____
_____
_____
_____

How does your thought life affect you? Where can your thoughts be coming from? How do you evaluate your thoughts correctly? (See page 109 of *Called to Truth, A Practical, Biblical Guide to Spiritual & Physical Wholeness*.)

_____
_____
_____
_____

According to Romans 12:2, what are the benefits of not conforming to the world?

_____
_____
_____
_____

d.) <u>Your Conscience</u>: What is the conscience?

_____
_____
_____

How does the conscience get seared (calloused, does not detect sin/evil)?

_____
_____
_____

How do you protect your conscience?

_____

_____

_____

FEAR AND ITS DANGERS

1. What are some of the emotions that can affect your body and soul negatively?

_____

_____

_____

_____

2. What casts out fear?

_____

_____

_____

_____

3. Once fear is cast out what do you need to be filled with?

_____

_____

_____

4. What do the lies of Satan do to your mind, body, and soul?

_____

_____

_____

5. Can you manage fear in your life, and why or why not?

_____

_____

_____

6. What are symptoms of the spirit of fear?

_____

_____

_____

7. According to First Peter 5:6-11, what are the acts of obedience you are to follow? What will be the result of your obedience?

_____

_____

_____

_____

_____

_____

8. What are some of the ways that fear gets access in your life?

_____

_____

_____

_____

_____

THE FULLNESS OF THE BELIEVER

After you have completed reading pages 112-115 of *Called to Truth, A Practical, Biblical Guide to Spiritual & Physical Wholeness*, answer the following questions:

Salvation

1. Write the words of John 3:16 below (also listed on page 112) and circle the word "believes." The word "believe" means "to make a commitment," "to trust," "to have faith in," and "to be persuaded of." Therefore, do you believe, make a commitment to, trust in, have faith in, and are persuaded that Jesus Christ, the Son of God, died for your sins, rose from the dead, and will return?

_____

_____

_____

_____

_____

_____

_____

_____

2. Write the words of Romans 10:9-10 below (also listed on page 112). There are five different main points from this verse. Therefore, using two different

colored highlighters alternate with a different color each separate point and then review the verse.

_____

_____

_____

_____

_____

_____

_____

3. After studying salvation on pages 112-113 of _Called to Truth, A Practical, Biblical Guide to Spiritual & Physical Wholeness_, journal in detail what it means to be born again.

_____

_____

_____

_____

_____

_____

_____

PRAYER TO CONFESS JESUS AS YOUR LORD AND SAVIOR (It is important to pray out loud because you are making a confession of what you believe.)

I confess with my mouth that the Lord Jesus is the Son of God. Jesus Christ died on the cross for my sins and the sins of the world. Jesus Christ resurrected from the dead and will return one day. I am a sinner who needs Jesus as my Lord and Savior. Second Corinthians 7:10 says godly sorrow works repentance to salvation. I repent and ask you to cleanse me of all unrighteousness according to First John 1:9.

According to Romans 10:10, "For with the heart man believes to righteousness; and with the mouth confession is made to salvation." Jesus come into my life and lead me!

PRAISE GOD FOR YOUR DECISION TO SERVE AND FOLLOW HIM WITH YOUR WHOLE HEART!

4. Use the space below to journal the scriptures that have revealed the love of Jesus Christ to you. Include in your journaling that you recognize you are a sinner who needs a Savior and that you believe Jesus Christ died for your sins, He is the Son of God, He has resurrected, and He will return one day. Read and confess your declarations out loud to Him.

_____

_____

_____

_____

_____

_____

_____

_____

_____

_____

_____

_____

_____

_____

_____

_____

_____

_____

5. What is an erring born again believer? What is the erring born again believer not to continue doing? What empowers the born again believer to overcome and not practice sinning?

_____

_____

_____

_____

_____

_____

6. According to the last paragraph on page 113 of *Called to Truth, A Practical, Biblical Guide to Spiritual & Physical Wholeness*, as sinners, how are you justified?

_____
_____
_____
_____
_____
_____
_____

7. Jesus was wounded for your transgressions. Jesus was bruised for your iniquities. Jesus took your punishment and brought you peace, and through His stripes (wounds) you are healed. Thanks be to God for our victory through our Lord Jesus Christ. By your faith, you receive what Jesus bought and paid for. By your faith in Jesus Christ, the Holy Spirit will empower you to obey Him and resist Satan. The Holy Spirit gives you the power, but you choose to obey. There is a choice involved where you say no to your fleshly desires and say yes to God and His ways. You choose to put aside the ways of this world and walk the narrow path to peace through Jesus Christ. The ways of this world lead to the wide path of destruction. Amid a crooked and perverse nation, according to Philippians 2, you work out your salvation with fear and trembling. Read Philippians 2:12-15 and study these verses in the Amplified version and the King James version. Then journal your understanding of these verses.

_____
_____
_____
_____
_____
_____
_____
_____
_____
_____
_____

Sanctification

THE PROCESS OF SANCTIFICATION IS VITAL TO THE BELIEVER'S WALK OF FAITH.

1. What is sanctification, why is it necessary to be sanctified, and how are you sanctified? Sanctification is to purify and to make holy. Sanctification is to be set apart for a purpose. As followers of Jesus Christ, you are set apart for God's plans and purposes. Your body is the temple of the Holy Spirit. You were bought with the blood of Jesus and are to keep your spirit, soul, and body from every evil thing. The God of peace sanctifies you wholly. He sanctifies your whole spirit, soul, and body. You are to bless God with your spirit, your mind, your will, your emotion, and your body. Are you allowing the imaginations of evil to ruminate in your mind; are you casting off evil thoughts? Do you have runaway emotions that are leading you into wrong decisions? Is your wounded soul making it difficult to hear the Holy Spirit? Are you keeping your body holy? These choices matter to God.

a.) In your own words, describe sanctification.

_____
_____
_____
_____
_____
_____
_____

2. Why is it necessary to be sanctified? The evil desires of the flesh can lead us into the wide road of destruction. The world and Satan's lies can deceive you if you are not seeking the LORD and His truth regularly and diligently. When you are heeding the correction of the LORD, when you fear the LORD and not man, when you are seeking His truths, and when you follow the lead of the Holy Spirit, you will be led to safety, delivered from evil, and moving in the direction of sanctification. When you are moving in the direction of sanctification, you learn to understand the spiritual laws and how you are either sowing into good or sowing into evil. Hebrews 10:26 states, *"For if we sin willfully after that we have received the knowledge of the truth, there remains no more sacrifice for sin."* As you choose to follow the Holy Spirit's lead and live by the word of God, you will be on the road of sanctification. Additional scripture to study Proverbs 1:22-33.

a.) Why is it necessary to be sanctified?

_____

_____

_____

_____

_____

_____

_____

3. First Timothy 4 reveals how some will leave the faith through listening to deceitful spirits and teachings of demons. You are to guard your heart and mind. When you are on the road of sanctification, you will be led into truth that sets you free and continually transforms you. Being sanctified and purified is a lifetime process. Once you have accepted Jesus as your Lord and Savior, this is only the beginning of your transformation and sanctification. Once you have received the gift of the Holy Spirit, you are then led by the Holy Spirit into obedience. Obedience to God is a lifestyle. The sanctification process gives us the power through the Holy Spirit to continue in obedience throughout our lifetime.

a.) After reading First Timothy 4:1, who can be deceived?

_____

_____

_____

b.) After reading First Timothy 4:1-16, how do you guard against being deceived?

_____

_____

4. How are you sanctified? Read and study each set of verses and take notes on the process of sanctification: Hebrews 9:13-15; First Peter 3:15; Second Timothy 2:21-26; John 17:17; Jeremiah 1:5; Hebrews 10:10; First Corinthians 1:2; Romans 15:16; Jude 1:1; Acts 20:32, and Acts 26:14-18.

_____

_____

_____

_____

_____

_____

_____

_____

_____

_____

_____

_____

_____

5. The purifying process of sanctification is a refining process which removes the impurities of sin. As God continues to purify you, you become more like Him. It is a place of peace and joy knowing you are moving according to His will for your life as you humble yourself in this process. Journal a testimony you have about yourself or someone else that clearly depicts the purifying process of sanctification.

_____

_____

_____

_____

_____

_____

_____

_____

_____

Baptism

Jesus spoke and said in Matthew 28:19-20, _"Go you therefore, and teach all nations, baptizing them in the name of the Father, and of the Son, and of the Holy Ghost. Teaching them to observe all things whatsoever I have commanded you. . ."_ Two things stand out to me as I study these verses. First, the teaching of the truth comes and then those who believe will be baptized. Second, Jesus instructs that those who are taught His truths are taught to observe them. Being water baptized is an action of love and obedience to His commands.

1. If you have not been water baptized and you have confessed Jesus as Lord and Savior of your life, I recommend reading page 114 of *Called to Truth, A Practical, Biblical Guide to Spiritual & Physical Wholeness*, studying First Peter 3:21; Ezekiel 36:25-27; Acts 22:16, and Colossians 2:12. As indicated in Acts 22:16, we are not to delay baptism. Journal your thoughts and prayers for revelatory truth on baptism.

_____

_____

_____

_____

_____

_____

_____

_____

_____

_____

2. Journal your baptism testimony.

_____

_____

_____

_____

_____

_____

Baptism of the Holy Spirit

Let's clarify the difference between water baptism and the baptism of the Holy Spirit. According to Matthew 3:11, John the Baptist spoke, *"I indeed baptize you with water to repentance: but He that comes after me is mightier than I, whose shoes I am not worthy to bear: He shall baptize you with the Holy Ghost, and with fire."* Furthermore, Jesus spoke in Acts 1:5, *"For John truly baptized with water; but you shall be baptized with the Holy Ghost not many days from now."*

The following is my testimony of the baptism of the Holy Spirit: I attended a ministry conference, and people who wanted prayer for the baptism of the Holy Spirit came forward. I went forward to be prayed over but my heart was not fully persuaded to receive. I had some unbelief about it. The next time I had an opportunity to receive was when I visited a healing room. The people there asked if I wanted the baptism of the Holy Spirit, and I indicated, "Yes!" I was fully persuaded; my whole heart was seeking God for truth and revelation in my life. The ministry team of two, anointed me with oil, laid hands on me, and prayed for the baptism of the Holy Spirit. I spoke in tongues shortly after. This day was a turning point for me because I was now fully immersed with the Holy Spirit. I began to have a deeper understanding of scripture, and I was now bold for the cause of Christ. I began walking in God's peace. No longer did the circumstances of life pull me down into the pit of darkness. The power of the Holy Spirit working through me was giving me the power and boldness to do His will in areas of my life where I struggled before. Second Timothy 1:7 states that God has given me a spirit of power and now I understood more completely what that meant. Furthermore, the gift of speaking in tongues powerfully edifies me and builds me up spiritually.

In Acts 4, verses 29-33, servants of the Lord were gathered in unity and prayed to the Lord for boldness to speak His word and that signs and wonders may be done in the name of Jesus. When they finished praying, the place was shaken, all were filled with the Holy Spirit, they spoke the word of God with boldness, great grace was on them all, and great power was given the apostles (messenger, an ambassador of the Gospel) to be witnesses of the resurrection of Jesus. Wow! Did you notice that after they received the baptism of the Holy Spirit, they now had the boldness and power to be witnesses of the resurrection of Jesus Christ?

1. If you have been baptized in the Holy Spirit, journal your testimony.

_____
_____
_____
_____
_____
_____
_____
_____

2. If you desire to receive the baptism of the Holy Spirit, read and meditate on the above scriptures, study Chapter 10, and study Acts 1:4-5, Acts 2:1-4, and Mark 16:17. Then pray in agreement with a follower of Jesus Christ for the baptism of the Holy Spirit, by the laying on of hands according to Second Timothy 1:6. If for some reason you cannot join with another believer in prayer, the prayer of faith avails much. I have a wonderful friend who spent a lot of time with the LORD in her prayer closet, and one day she was

overcome by the Holy Spirit's power and began speaking in tongues shortly after. Journal your prayer and scriptures on these truths.

_____

_____

_____

_____

_____

_____

_____

_____

3. If you do not want the baptism of the Holy Spirit, journal your thoughts about this. God wants you to be truthful when you talk to Him so explain your doubt or unbelief to Him.

_____

_____

_____

_____

<u>The Lord's Supper (Holy Communion)</u>

The Lord's Supper is the New Covenant which is an agreement. When you partake of the Lord's Supper, you are coming into agreement and remembrance of Jesus Christ's death, burial, and resurrection; you are proclaiming the Lord's death until He returns. Isaiah 53:5 states, *"But He was wounded for our transgressions, He was bruised for our iniquities: the chastisement of our peace was upon Him; and with His stripes we are healed."* (It is important to understand the significance of the Lord's Supper, and we will look at this further.)

We will study First Corinthians 11:24-34 in the Amplified version: *"And when He had given thanks, He broke it and said, 'This is (represents) My body, which is [offered as a sacrifice] for you. Do this in [affectionate] remembrance of Me.' In the same way, after supper He took the cup, saying, 'This cup is the new covenant [ratified and established] in My blood; do this, as often as you drink it, in [affectionate] remembrance of Me.' For every time you eat this bread and drink this cup, you are [symbolically] proclaiming [the fact of] the Lord's death until He comes [again]. So when whoever eats the bread or drinks the cup of the Lord in a way that is unworthy [of Him] will be guilty of [profaning and sinning against] the body and blood of the Lord. But a person must [prayerfully] examine himself [and his relationship to Christ], and only when he has done so should he eat of the bread and drink of the cup. For anyone who eats and drinks [without solemn reverence and heartfelt gratitude for the sacrifice of Christ], eats and drinks a judgment on himself if he does not recognize the body [of Christ]. That [careless and unworthy participation] is the reason why many among you are weak and sick, and a number sleep [in death]. But if we evaluated and judged ourselves honestly [recognizing our shortcomings and correcting our behavior], we would not be judged. But when we [fall short and] are judged by the Lord, we are disciplined [by undergoing His correction] so that we will not be condemned [to eternal punishment] along with the world. So then, my brothers and sisters, when you come together to eat [the Lord's Supper], wait for one another [and see to it that no one is left out]. If anyone is too hungry [to wait], let him eat at home, so that you will not come together for judgment [on yourselves]. About the remaining matters [of which I was informed], I will take care of them when I come."* It would also bring further clarity to read these verses in the King James Version.

In summary, it is therefore important that you examine yourself, examine your relationship with Jesus, have heartfelt gratitude for Christ's sacrifice, and understand and recognize the significance of the Lord's Supper before taking the Lord's Supper. No one should be coming to the Lord's Supper to satisfy their hunger for food or drink. Many are weak and sick; a number of people sleep because of their careless partaking of the Lord's Supper. It is a heart issue; God is looking at the heart and the state of your heart is imperative. Being in the word of God and studying the verses on the Lord's Supper will bring revelation.

1. Journal the significance of the Lord's Supper and the importance in examining yourself before partaking.

_____

_____

_____

_____

_____

_____

_____

_____

2. Notice in the above scripture verses of First Corinthians 11 that it explains we are to judge ourselves honestly, recognize our shortcomings, and correct our behavior. According to these verses, what happens if we don't do this?

_____
_____
_____
_____
_____
_____

Greatest Commandment

1. The first and great commandment is to love the LORD with all your heart, with all your soul, and with all your mind. The second is to love your neighbor as yourself.

Do you love the LORD with all your heart, with all your thoughts, and with all your will? The word "all" means completely, throughout, ultimately, and whole. To test this, examine your heart and who you are desiring to please.

When you are making decisions, do you determine if they are pleasing to God? Journal your thoughts.

_____

2. Do you love yourself and do your thoughts and actions towards yourself reveal that?

_____
_____
_____
_____
_____
_____
_____

3. Do you love your neighbor (others you encounter)? What do your thoughts and actions toward others reveal?

_____
_____
_____

_____
_____
_____
_____

Forgiveness

1. After reading and studying pages 22 and 29 of *Called to Truth, A Practical, Biblical Guide to Spiritual & Physical Wholeness*, continue reading and completing this section. Forgiveness is a choice and unforgiveness has a dangerous consequence. Who are you hurting by holding onto unforgiveness in your soul (from page 29 and Matthew 18)?

_____
_____

2. Is forgiveness from the heart or the head?

_____
_____

3. Who is the Judge of all mankind?

_____
_____

4. What are the consequences if you don't forgive?

_____
_____

5. How do you know if you have truly forgiven someone?

_____
_____

6. According to Mark 11:25, *"And when you stand praying, forgive, if you **have anything against any**: that your Father also which is in heaven **may forgive you your trespasses**."* According to this verse what type of offenses are you to forgive, and who are you to forgive?

_____
_____

7. In addition, according to Mark 11:25, when we have forgiven anyone of anything, what does Our Father in heaven do?

_____

_____

8. What is your responsibility, according to Matthew 5:23-24, if someone has a complaint or grievance against you?

_____

_____

9. According to Psalm 97:10, Romans 12:9, and Proverbs 8:13, what are you to hate?

_____

_____

10. Examine your heart and determine if you are holding unforgiveness in your heart. Are you holding unforgiveness towards yourself, God, or another person? Journal your heart felt thoughts and prayer. If your heart has made the choice to forgive someone, release that person from your soul (call them out of your belly by name).

_____

_____

_____

_____

_____

_____

_____

_____

_____

_____

_____

_____

Walking by Faith

If we are only living by our circumstances and never activate our faith, how will our circumstances change? When the disciple Peter stepped out of the boat and walked on the water, He trusted Jesus. When we exercise our faith by stepping out of the boat to walk on water, we will begin to see evidence of change in our life. Living a life of faith is exciting and freeing because we are trusting God, not ourselves. We are not believing in our efforts to achieve something but in what Jesus has done and says in His word.

When Peter became afraid and began to sink in the water, Jesus said, *"O you of little faith, wherefore did you doubt?"* Doubt and unbelief bring fear. When we continue to keep our eyes and focus on Jesus and not ourselves and not our circumstances, we will overcome fear, doubt, and unbelief. <u>Faith isn't about us trusting ourselves to accomplish something. It is about trusting Him with our life!</u>

1. Journal the evidence in your life that you are trusting God, not yourself. Then journal the evidence where you are <u>not</u> trusting God but trusting yourself.

_____

_____

_____

_____

_____

_____

_____

_____

_____

_____

_____

2. Where is God asking you to step out of the boat and walk on water (walk by faith)?

_____

_____

_____

_____

_____

_____

_____

_____

3. To have faith is to be fully persuaded. Faith comes by hearing and hearing by the word of God. The more truth you understand for yourself, the more your faith is purified and grows because it is planted on good ground. Believing lies will infect your faith with doubt and unbelief. If you do not understand or believe a scripture for yourself, your faith cannot produce fruit. Journal your thoughts and prayer about being fully persuaded (faith) in the word of God. List any scriptures you do not understand or have revelation of and are seeking God for understanding.

_____
_____
_____
_____
_____
_____
_____
_____
_____
_____
_____
_____

Be not conformed to this world

To conform is to be similar by following the same pattern or fashion. Do you look like everyone else living according to the world or do you act and behave like Jesus? According to First John 2:15, *"Love not the world, neither the things that are in the world. If any man loves the world, the love of the Father is not in him."*

How do you keep from conforming to the world? Romans 12:2 says by renewing your mind you will be able to prove what is good, acceptable, and the perfect will of God. When your mind is renewed by the word of God, you will be transformed and have the mind of Christ.

1. Are you following the same patterns as the world?

_____

_____

2. Do you love the things of this world or are your eyes on your first love, Jesus?

_____

_____

3. What you are saying and doing will reveal who you are following and conforming to. Examine your heart; in what areas of your life are you seeking the world's advice, and in what areas of your life are you seeking God's advice? Journal the areas of your life that you are following the world's views and the areas of your life that you are following Jesus.

_____

_____

_____

_____

_____

_____

_____

_____

_____

_____

Obedience to the LORD. The Holy Spirit leads us to repentance.

As God's children, you are called to be obedient to His laws and commands. As a believer of Jesus Christ, the Holy Spirit leads you into all truth and empowers you to be obedient. By listening and obeying the Holy Spirit, you will put to death the deeds of the body and live. Those that are led by the Holy Spirit, they are the sons of God (Romans 8). Furthermore, John 14:26 explains that the Father will send the Holy Spirit to you to teach you all things and bring all things to your remembrance.

1. Examine your walk with the Lord. Are you hearing and obeying the Holy Spirit?

_____

_____

2. Are you choosing to ignore the promptings of the Holy Spirit?

_____

_____

_____

3. Has your conscience been seared (scorched, charred) by continual sinning so that you no longer detect right from wrong and cannot hear the promptings of the Holy Spirit?

_____

_____

_____

4. Are you experiencing oppression and thus have difficulty hearing the promptings of the Holy Spirit?

_____

_____

_____

_____

5. There is no condemnation as a believer in Jesus Christ, but the Holy Spirit (Spirit of Truth) leads us into all truth. For further revelation, you can read and study John 14 and Romans 8 and journal your notes below. If you are not hearing the promptings of the Holy Spirit, keep seeking truths from scripture and ask God to show you the barrier that is blocking you from hearing the promptings of the Holy Spirit.

_____

_____

_____

_____

_____

_____

_____

_____

_____

_____

Submit yourself to God. Resist the devil.

Pride and arrogance are man's downfall but humbling yourself before the LORD is extremely powerful! When you come with humility before God, you will learn truths from Him that will set you free from the bondage of Satan and from the bondage of the fear of man. Fearing man is a trap, but those who trust God will be safe. The world tries to get us to trust its fallen ways for our safety. Our true protection, however, is in submitting to God.

Resist means to withstand, oppose, refuse to be moved, hold one's ground, and strongly combat an opponent. You are to oppose the devil. You are not to sit back and watch him attack you. I had a vision that I was in a boxing ring, against the ropes, just letting the devil attack me. I needed to get my boxing gloves on in the spiritual realm and resist Satan with spiritual warfare, prayer, speaking life with my mouth, declaring scripture, and confronting evil in the physical realm by my words of truth. Satan is going to attack because that is what he does; he steals, he kills, and he destroys. My responsibility as a follower of Jesus Christ was (and is) to gear up with knowledge of the truth and use my authority to remove Satan out of my life. You are responsible for your life and resisting evil.

1. Journal your plan and steps to submit yourself to God and resist the devil.

_____

_____

_____

_____

_____

_____

_____

_____

_____

_____

Abiding in the LORD. Abide is to remain and to continue in relationship.

1. In any important relationship, you will spend quality time with that person, and you will plan and prepare for your time with them. The LORD wants you to have personal experiences with Him and have a testimony of His goodness in your life. What do you want to plan and include in your life that

you love doing with the LORD and for the LORD? The following are some suggestions: studying scripture; praise and worship; prayer; intercessory prayer; Bible studies; listening to biblical teachings; attending church; serving the needy; including Him in every part of your day; preparing yourself for your divine calling; using the gifts He has given you, or simply be alone with the LORD, whether it be a walk in the forest, prayer closet, etc. Journal your intentional plans to abide in the LORD.

_____

_____

_____

_____

_____

_____

_____

_____

_____

_____

2. Jeremiah 29:13 says, *"And you shall seek Me, and find Me, when you shall search for Me with all your heart."* When you search for Him with all your heart, you will find Him. How will you search for the LORD with all your heart?

_____

_____

_____

_____

_____

_____

_____

_____

_____

_____

Prayer and fasting

1. After carefully reading Isaiah 58:1-12, describe the correct attitude of the heart when praying and fasting.

_____
_____
_____
_____
_____
_____
_____
_____
_____

2. According to verse 6 of Isaiah 58, what are the breakthroughs manifested from fasting?

_____
_____
_____
_____
_____
_____
_____
_____

3. After careful examination of Isaiah 58:7-10, what will your actions be when you are fasting with your whole heart and following the principles of Isaiah 58?

_____
_____
_____
_____
_____
_____
_____
_____

4. According to verses 8-12 of Isaiah 58, what are the blessings of fasting?

_____
_____
_____

_____
_____
_____
_____
_____
_____
_____
_____

Praising God

1. To praise someone means to recognize their good acts and express gratitude. Who are you praising for their good acts?

_____
_____
_____
_____

2. According to Psalm 96:

      a.) Who are the idols?

_____
_____
_____
_____

      b.) Who are you to declare His glory to?

_____
_____
_____

      c.) Journal the reasons Our Heavenly Father is to be praised.

_____
_____
_____
_____

3. Worship is to adore, show reverence, and to fall down before. According to John 4:23-24, how are you to worship Him?

_____

_____

_____

You reap what you sow.

Read and meditate on Galatians 6:4-10. What seed the farmer will plant is the crop he will harvest. With the seeds you are planting now, what will you harvest? Evaluate the seeds you are sowing in your life. Will you be reaping a beautiful harvest or a destructive crop? Reaping what you sow is a spiritual law that will play out in your life whether you are sowing good or bad seed.

1. First, evaluate what seeds you are sowing in your life. Are you sowing seeds of faith, obedience, speaking words of life, casting off evil imaginations, casting off worries and trusting God, using your hands for good, blessing someone else's life, prayer, etc.? Journal your evaluation of the seeds you are sowing.

_____
_____
_____
_____
_____
_____
_____
_____
_____
_____

2. Second, are you nourishing the seeds you planted? If you have planted good seed but have not yet produced a harvest, evaluate what you can do to nourish those seeds that haven't manifested a harvest in your life or someone else's life. For in due season, you will reap. Journal your plan to nourish the seeds that have not yet harvested. Examples would be prayer and fasting, praying in tongues, or seeking God for wisdom for the situation.

_____
_____

_____

_____

_____

_____

_____

3. Third, each of us is responsible for our own life and for what we do with our time here on earth. You will reap what you sow, and if you commit your ways to the LORD, He will direct your path. According to the principles from Proverbs 3:4-5, the LORD will direct your path when: you trust the LORD with all your heart, you do not lean on your own understanding, and in all your ways acknowledge Him. Acknowledge means "to tell" or "to confess." Thereby, telling the LORD about your ways and committing your ways to Him. Tell the LORD by journaling what you are acknowledging Him in, trusting Him about, and leaning not on your own understanding.

_____

_____

_____

_____

_____

_____

_____

_____

_____

⚓ Truth Basic Training Verses

Carefully study the following verses by reading the scripture in various translations, including the King James Version; underline any words that stand out to you; use a Strong's Concordance, which is an index of every word in the King James Version, and read the entire chapter of the verse. Journal your notes and summary.

"My people are destroyed for lack of knowledge: because thou hast rejected knowledge, I will also reject thee, that thou shalt be no priest to me: seeing thou hast forgotten the law of thy God, I will also forget thy children." Hosea 4:6

_____

_____

_____

_____
_____
_____
_____
_____

"My son, forget not my law; but let thine heart keep my commandments: For length of days, and long life, and peace, shall they add to thee." Proverbs 3:1-2

_____
_____
_____
_____
_____
_____

"Be not wise in thine own eyes: fear the LORD, and depart from evil. It shall be health to thy navel, and marrow to thy bones." Proverbs 3:7-8

_____
_____
_____
_____
_____
_____

CHAPTER 19

---❧---

LAYING ON OF HANDS

God's hands laid the foundation of the earth and his right hand spread out the heavens. Jesus sits at the right hand of the power of God. God's right hand sustains us. The right hand of the LORD exalts. The LORD's right hand broke the enemy in pieces.

What are you to do with your hands? You are to bless. You are to help. You are to love. You are to heal, and you are to break apart the power of evil.

👣 YOUR JOURNEY TO TRUTH

What we do with our hands and the position of our hands can reveal truth about what is going on inside of us. As my walk with the LORD was growing and I was learning to trust God completely, I noticed my position in worshipping Him was different. In my old style of worship, I would keep my hands to my sides. But as I was attending a church where people raised their hands in worship, seeing fellow believers have this position in worship was new to me. One time I wanted to express my love to God, and it felt natural to raise my hands. I soon loved to raise my hands in worship, and it was very freeing to me; I felt it was an expression of trusting God with my whole heart. Something about the position of worship with my uplifted hands revealed to me that I was trusting Him with my whole heart. It was a display of my openness to share with Him and experience a relationship of love and trust with Him. It was kind of like hugging someone. You don't usually hug someone you aren't close to, and I felt close to God and wanted to show Him I trusted Him with by entire being. Your hands can hold people back that you don't trust or draw people in that you do trust.

AND THESE SIGNS SHALL FOLLOW THEM THAT BELIEVE . . .THEY SHALL LAY HANDS ON THE SICK

1. After reading Chapter 19 of *Called to Truth, A Practical, Biblical Guide to Spiritual & Physical Wholeness* and the included scriptures, what is the "laying on of hands" for?

_____
_____
_____
_____
_____
_____
_____
_____

2. The laying on of hands should be done with care. Explain this statement according to First Timothy 5:22 and Second John 11 (Read the entire chapter to bring further clarity).

_____
_____
_____
_____
_____
_____
_____
_____

Therefore, it is important to use our wisdom and discernment as to who lays hands on us and whom we lay hands on.

3. Why would you lay hands on yourself?

_____
_____
_____
_____
_____

_____

_____

All things as a believer are to be done in faith or there is no effect. The laying on of hands on oneself and others is to be done in faith.

⚓ Truth Basic Training Verses

Carefully study the following verses by reading the scripture in various translations, including the King James Version; underline any words that stand out to you; use a Strong's Concordance, which is an index of every word in the King James Version, and read the entire chapter of the verse. Journal your notes and summary.

"And they went forth, and preached everywhere, the Lord working with them, and confirming the word with signs following. Amen." Mark 16:20 (see Mark 16:15-20)

_____

_____

_____

_____

_____

_____

_____

"Wherefore I put you in remembrance that you stir up the gift of God, which is in you by the putting on of my hands." 2 Timothy 1:6

_____

_____

_____

_____

_____

_____

CHAPTER 20

———— ❦ ————

RELATIONSHIPS BUILT ON SOLID GROUND

Before we can have relationships built on solid ground, we need to have a relationship with the Lord Jesus Christ. Our relationship with Him is our most important relationship. We will be on solid ground when we are connected to the true vine because we will be branches of Him. Through our relationship with Jesus and His word we will learn to handle our relationship according to His ways.

When you understand and receive your Heavenly Father's love, you will be able to speak and receive truth in your relationships. When you take an offense in relationships, you are receiving the offense. As you release offenses (hurts) to God, He will lead you to "The Way," "The Truth," and "The Life" for your relationships. Come along on **Your Journey to Truth** to building your relationships on solid ground.

👣 YOUR JOURNEY TO TRUTH

Before completing the below checklist, read Chapter 20 of *Called to Truth, A Practical, Biblical Guide to Spiritual & Physical Wholeness.*

The checklist below is a guideline to examine yourself and evaluate if you love yourself and others. The more checkmarks you have, the more you are moving towards loving yourself and others the way God desires you to love.

Before you begin this checklist, be honest with yourself and glean as much information as you can through evaluating each point according to how that attribute of love was tested through a difficult situation. For example, if your husband received a new car from his company, but you must continue driving a perfectly working but 15-year-old car, would you be envious or jealous about him having a brand-new beautiful car or happy for him? Answering these questions with thorough evaluation of yourself is going to give you a valuable tool.

1. Checklist: Do I love according to First Corinthians 13:4-7?

_____Love suffers long (love is patient)

_____Love is kind (love is thoughtful)

_____Love does not envy (love is not jealous)

_____Love does not parade itself (love does not brag)

_____Love is not puffed up (love is not proud or arrogant)

_____Love does not behave rude

_____Love does not seek its own (love is not self-seeking)

_____Love is not provoked (love is not overly sensitive and not easily angered)

_____Love thinks no evil (it does not consider a wrong endured)

_____Love does not rejoice in iniquity (it does not rejoice at injustice)

_____Love rejoices in the truth

_____Love bears all things

_____Love believes all things

_____Love hopes all things

_____Love endures all things

2. After reading page 121 of *Called to Truth, A Practical, Biblical Guide to Spiritual & Physical Wholeness* (additional reading page 16-17), journal God's order in the family and God's order in marriage.

_____

_____

_____

_____
_____
_____
_____
_____
_____

After studying God's order in the family and marriage, what, if anything, is out of order in your family or marriage? (refer to page 16-17 and page 121 of *Called to Truth, A Practical, Biblical Guide to Spiritual & Physical Wholeness*)

_____
_____
_____
_____

What problems can come from being outside of God's order regarding marriage and family? (refer to page 16-17 and 121 of *Called to Truth, A Practical, Biblical Guide to Spiritual & Physical Wholeness*)

_____
_____
_____
_____

If your family or marriage is not in order according to God's divine order, pray and ask God for wisdom in restoring order.

3. This checklist is a guide to help evaluate your close relationships (spouse or others) and their possible negative effects on your wholeness.

"YOU SHALL NOT PLOW WITH AN OX AND AN ASS TOGETHER." Deut.22:10

_____A relationship where someone is not a follower of Jesus Christ

_____A relationship where someone is being led into evil

_____A relationship where someone manipulates or tries to control the other

_____A relationship where someone is jealous or envious of the other

_____A relationship where someone is putting that relationship before God

_____A relationship where someone is continually avoiding the truth and never works on solving problems

_____A relationship where someone is prideful or arrogant and unwilling to be humble

_____A relationship where someone is unreliable or untrustworthy

_____A relationship where someone is sexually immoral

_____A relationship where someone gossips

_____A relationship where someone is fake or not authentic

_____A relationship where love (described above) is not present

_____A relationship where both are not likeminded

_____A relationship where strife (conflict) continually exists with no resolution

_____A relationship where someone is lying, cheating, or deceiving the other

_____A relationship where neither person edifies (improves) the other

_____A relationship where neither person brings wisdom or good judgment to the other

4. Examining ourselves and our relationships can save us from making bad decisions in our life and straying off course. We can remove some relationships from our lives, but we can't with some others. Therefore, it is important to seek God for guidance in how to navigate the relationships you have and for wisdom about the ones you need to remove from your life. <u>Journal below the most important people in your life that influence your behavior, and how their actions and behavior effect your life</u>. Pray and seek God's guidance for your relationships.

_____
_____
_____
_____
_____
_____
_____
_____

_____
_____
_____
_____
_____
_____
_____
_____
_____

5. Journal your creative strategies to navigate the challenging relationships in your life.

_____
_____
_____
_____
_____
_____
_____
_____
_____
_____
_____
_____
_____
_____
_____
_____
_____
_____

⚓ Truth Basic Training Verses

Carefully study the following verses by reading the scripture in various translations, including the King James Version; underline any words that stand out to you; use a Strong's Concordance, which is an index of every word in the King James Version, and read the entire chapter of the verse. Journal your notes and summary.

"Be you not unequally yoked together with unbelievers: for what fellowship has righteousness with unrighteousness? And what communion has light with darkness?" 2 Corinthians 6:14

_____
_____
_____
_____
_____
_____
_____
_____
_____
_____

CHAPTER 21

TRUTH CHANGES FACT

With truth, people-pleasers transform into God-pleasers. With truth, liars transform into truth speakers. With truth, talebearers transform into encouragers. With truth, fear-filled people transform into believers who are bold as lions for Christ. With the truth spoken out of Margy Mayfield's mouth, serial killer Stephen Morin came to Christ, and Stephen brought others to Christ while he was in prison. Stephen Morin was executed by lethal injection in Texas in 1985.

Margy had a book of scripture with her when she was abducted by Stephen. With the love of Jesus Christ and the word of God, Margy witnessed to Stephen, and it transformed a serial killer's soul from death to life. Margy visited Stephen at the prison before he was executed, and Stephen told her how he heard the audible voice of God when she had witnessed to him when he abducted her. When Stephen heard the audible voice of God say that this was the last time He (God) was going to call Stephen, Stephen raised his hands, responding to God's call.

God uses us to speak truth to others. Through Margy's obedience to God, the day she was abducted, and her carefully following the Holy Spirit's leading, she was used by God to speak words of life to Stephen that day. Stephen had never experienced love on this earth until he had the encounter with Margy. Margy ministered to Stephen for hours by sharing the truth of God's love and the scriptures she knew in her heart. When we are willing to be used by God, we will witness the power of God and how He changes people's destinies when they say yes to His call. (Seek4Truth Podcast, Margy Mayfield Abduction Testimony)

Come along on **Your Journey to Truth** and see how "The Way," "The Truth," and "The Life" changes the facts.

👣 YOUR JOURNEY TO TRUTH

Before answering the below questions, read Chapter 21 of *Called to Truth, A Practical, Biblical Guide to Spiritual & Physical Wholeness.*

<u>SEEK TRUTH AND BE FREE</u>

Evil tried to destroy "The Way," "The Truth," and "The Life," but Jesus Christ of Nazareth rose from His death of crucifixion to ultimately sitting at the right hand of God. Evil will use all means to destroy truth, but when truth showed up through the life and victory of Jesus Christ, Satan's principalities and powers were disarmed and Jesus was triumphantly victorious over Satan's evil kingdom. You are also to disarm Satan from having access to your life by using the authority given to you through the completed work of Jesus Christ. Your faith has an assignment to walk out the truth in your life! You choose!

You will find your "Life" when you seek "Truth" with all your heart. When God's supernatural power shows up, our current facts or current reality are transformed into His transforming "Truth" in our lives.

1. Read Luke 13:11-13, and you will see how "Truth" changed 18 years of facts in one woman's life. Journal the facts in this woman's life and then record what "Truth" changed her life.

_____
_____
_____
_____
_____
_____
_____
_____
_____
_____
_____

2. Read Luke 8:43-48 and journal the facts of this woman's life and then the "Truth" that changed her life.

_____
_____
_____
_____
_____
_____
_____
_____
_____
_____

3. According to Joel 2:25, "*And I will restore to you the years that the locust hath eaten, the cankerworm, and the caterpillar, and the palmerworm, my great army which I sent among you.*" Locusts are known for forming enormous swarms that devour crops and cause serious damage. The cankerworm is an inchworm whose infestations come in cycles and certain types of trees draw these worms. The caterpillar's name means the ravager, which means destruction, damage, or harm. The palmerworm name means to devour. The devouring, ravaging enemy may have stolen years of your life, but the LORD restores the lost years, and His word restores. What has the enemy stolen from you that you are seeking the LORD for restoration?

_____
_____
_____
_____
_____
_____
_____
_____
_____
_____
_____
_____
_____

4. The word of God says, "*Ask, and it shall be given; seek, and you shall find; knock, and it shall be opened to you.*" What are your plans to actively continue to seek truth in your life?

_____
_____
_____
_____
_____
_____
_____
_____
_____
_____
_____

5. After reading the final paragraph on pages 127-128 of _Called to Truth, A Practical, Biblical Guide to Spiritual & Physical Wholeness_, answer the following questions: Are you willing to let God lead you into unknown territory where you are seeking His will for your life?

_____
_____
_____
_____
_____
_____
_____
_____
_____

6. How have you grown spiritually through this study guide, and in what areas are you continuing to seek God for spiritual truth and revelation?

_____
_____
_____
_____
_____
_____
_____

_____

_____

⚓ Truth Basic Training Verses

Carefully study the following verses by reading the scripture in various translations, including the King James Version; underline any words that stand out to you; use a Strong's Concordance, which is an index of every word in the King James Version, and read the entire chapter of the verse. Journal your notes and summary.

"Sanctify them through thy truth: thy word is truth." John 17:17

_____

_____

_____

_____

_____

_____

"And you shall know the truth, and the truth shall make you free." John 8:32

_____

_____

_____

_____

_____

_____

"God is Spirit: and they that worship Him must worship Him in spirit and in truth." John 4:24

_____

_____

_____

_____

_____

_____

_____

_____

Your Journey to Truth

"By humility and the fear of the LORD are riches, and honor, and life." Proverbs 22:4

_____
_____
_____
_____
_____
_____

👣 YOUR JOURNEY TO TRUTH

Continues as you seek the LORD with all your heart.

BIBLIOGRAPHY

Beard, Steve. "The winding path to Graceland: Elvis Presley's spiritual quest." January 2002. Thunderstruck.org. (Steve Beard's article was adapted from "Defending Elvis" by Risen Magazine)

Biblegateway.com. Amplified Bible.

Biblegateway.com. King James Version.

Biblehub.com NAS Exhaustive Concordance of the Bible with Hebrew-Aramaic and Greek Dictionaries. The Lockman Foundation. 1998.

Biblehub.com. Strong's Concordance. Helps Word-studies. Helps Ministries, Inc. 2011.

Biblehub.com. Thayer's Greek Lexicon, Electronic Database. Biblesoft, Inc. 2011.

Blair, Elizabeth. "The Real 'Hacksaw Ridge' Soldier Saved 75 Souls Without Ever Carrying A Gun." November 4, 2016. NPR.org.

Brooks, Steven. How to Operate in the Gifts of the Spirit. Shippensburg, PA: Destiny Image Publishers, Inc. 2014.

Burden, Ralph. "Elvis Presley." Reallifestories.org.

Ewing, Minister Kevin L.A. "Understanding the Mystery of Fasting." YouTube.

"Forgiveness Letting Go of Grudges and Bitterness." Healthy Lifestyle Adult Health. Mayo Foundation for Medical Education & Research. 2019.

"Forgiveness: Your Health Depends On It." John Hopkins Medicine. 2019.

GodRules.net. KJV Strong's Concordance.

King James Version Easy Reading Bible. Goodyear, AZ: The Publisher. 2002.

Mayfield, Margy. "Margy Mayfield Abduction Testimony." SEEK4TRUTHPODCASTS. YouTube.

Oxford English Dictionary. Oxford Languages.

Price, Frederick K. C. Answered Prayer Guaranteed. Lake Mary, Florida: Charisma House. 2006.

Prince, Derek. They Shall Expel Demons. Grand Rapids, MI: Chosen Books. 1998.

Scrivner, Thurman. The Living Savior Ministries. CD Healing Teachings. Justin, TX.

Smith, Michael W. HardcoreChristianity.com. YouTube Deliverance Training Videos. Sun City, AZ.

"The Deadly Consequences of Unforgiveness." Lorie Johnson. CBN News. June 22, 2015.

Winston, Dr. Bill. Transform Your Thinking, Transform Your Life. Tulsa, OK: Harrison House, Inc. 2008.

"Wisconsin Native Molly Seidel Takes Bronze in Women's Marathon." August 7, 2021. The Associated Press. wearegreenbay.com

Wommack, Andrew. The New You and the Holy Spirit. Colorado Springs, CO: Andrew Wommack Industries, Inc. 2012.

Wright, Dr. Henry W. A More Excellent Way. New Kensington, PA: Whitaker House. 2009.

ABOUT AUTHOR

DENISE WHITE has been married for 31 years and has two children. Denise is a follower of Jesus Christ. Her faith has brought her peace and victory. Denise has a B.S. Degree and is a member of Delta Mu Delta. She has enjoyed her career in educating children. Denise's ministries have included ministering in the marketplace, children's groups, homeless women, and foster care ministry.

ABOUT KHARIS PUBLISHING

Kharis Publishing, an imprint of Kharis Media LLC, is a leading Christian and inspirational book publisher focused on inspirational and faith-based books. The dual mission of Kharis Publishing is to give voice to underrepresented writers (including women and first-time authors) and equip orphans in developing countries with literacy tools. That is why, for each book sold, the publisher channels some of the proceeds into providing books and computers for orphanages in developing countries, so these kids may learn to read, dream, and grow. Learn more at: https://www.kharispublishing.com/kp. For a limited time, Kharis Publishing welcomes unsolicited submission (inspirational and Christian nonfiction).

www.ingramcontent.com/pod-product-compliance
Lightning Source LLC
Chambersburg PA
CBHW051420090426
42737CB00014B/2759